Business Management for Standard Grade

Alan Bryce and Jamieson Wilson

Heinemann Educational Publishers,
Halley Court, Jordan Hill, Oxford OX2 8EJ
A division of Reed Educational & Professional Publishing Ltd

Heinemann is a registered trademark of Reed Educational & Professional
Publishing Limited

OXFORD MELBOURNE AUCKLAND JOHANNESBURG BLANTYRE
GABORONE IBADAN PORTSMOUTH NH (USA) CHICAGO

First published 2002
2006 2005 2004 2003 2002
10 9 8 7 6 5 4 3 2 1

A catalogue record for this book is available from the British Library on
request.

ISBN 0 435 45548 6

Pages designed by Artistix, Thame, Oxon

Typeset and illustrated by TechType, Abingdon, Oxon

Printed and bound in Great Britain by Scotprint, East Lothian

Tel: 01865 888058 www.heinemann.co.uk

Contents

Section 3 The resources businesses use

Acknowledgements

The authors and publisher would like to thank the following organisations for permission to reproduce extracts and other copyright material:

Associated Press
BMW
British Broadcasting Corporation
Corbis
East Ayrshire Council
Inventors World Magazine
Mary Evans Picture Library
Microsoft® Encarta® Online Encyclopedia 2002
Scottish Enterprise
The Stockmarket
Sue Cunningham
Thomas Cook
Wilson Sporting Goods Co.

Every effort has been made to contact copyright holders of material reproduced in this book. We would be glad to hear from unacknowledged sources at the first opportunity.

Websites

Please note that the examples of websites suggested in this book were up to date at the time of writing. It is essential for tutors to preview each site before using it to ensure that the URL is still accurate and the content is appropriate. We suggest that tutors bookmark useful sites and consider enabling students to access them through the school or college intranet.

Introduction

This book has been designed to help you prepare for your Standard Grade Business Management course. There are four sections:

Section 1: What is a business?
Section 2: How do businesses develop and perform?
Section 3: The resources businesses use
Section 4: How businesses are managed

These sections mirror the four 'official' Areas of Study as laid down by the Scottish Qualifications Authority. Each of these sections is divided into units, covering all of the essential topics you need to know about to complete the course successfully.

The following elements are key features of the book:

- checklist of topics at the beginning of each unit
- case studies
- test your knowledge and understanding
- test your decision-making skills
- activities to develop key skills such as communication and IT
- did you know?

Throughout the book, you are provided with a range of practical activities that will help you to apply your knowledge to real-life business situations. As you progress through the units, you will develop the necessary knowledge and skills that will help you to understand and contribute to the ever-changing world of business.

This book will also prepare you for the external examination by testing your ability to recall knowledge and, by analysing and interpreting data, to make quality decisions.

Business Management for Standard Grade provides a range of opportunities for real-life experiences both in and beyond the classroom. We wish you every success in your Business Management for Standard Grade course!

Section 1

What is a business?

- What do businesses do?
- Why do businesses exist?
- How are businesses organised?

UNIT 1 / What do businesses do?

In this unit you will learn about:

- providing a range of goods and services
- satisfying needs and wants
- small and large businesses
- private and public businesses
- primary, secondary and tertiary production
- production and consumption
- creating wealth.

1.1 / What you really, really want!

In the 1990s, a pop group used the song line 'what you really, really want'. This covers the very first facts the business world has to deal with.

We all have **needs** – water, food, shelter, and clothes – and for different reasons, we cannot live without them. No water and we die after four or five days; no food and we die after a few months. Shelter and clothes depend on climate and location. A mansion with walls three feet thick would be very useful on the Atlantic coast of Scotland but a cardboard box house might be too much on the Mediterranean coast of Greece. In Europe, clothing has been used for centuries, but it varies greatly between the Arctic Circle in Norway and the Sicilian coast town of Syracuse. In Africa, on the equator, clothing is minimal and follows social, rather than 'life', needs.

We all have **wants** as well as needs. These are extra things that make life more enjoyable such as fashion clothes, a yacht, winning the lottery, a car, makeup, or a WAP phone. None of these goods or services keeps us alive, but they make life more lively and stimulating. Some wants have become essentials such as telephones, washing machines and televisions.

Businesses exist to look after (or 'satisfy') these wants, whether it is by making better motorways, encouraging you to gamble on the National Lottery, buying the new style of shoe, supporting voluntary bodies like Amnesty International or Greenpeace, or flying faster, further and cheaper on holiday.

Is it a good or a service?

Every product that you can see or touch is a **good** and all other products are **services**. Food is a good; 'caring for the homeless' is a service. In your classroom, some goods are books, desks, chairs, and pencils. Electricity and teachers, on the other hand, are services.

Goods can be described in different ways:

- *non-durable* – goods that can only be used once; for consumers
- *durable* – goods that eventually wear out or break (e.g. bed, video-recorder, hair brush); for consumers
- *industrial* – goods that help to produce other goods e.g. machinery, cranes; for businesses.

As noted above, services are non-physical products and it is important that you know that well over *half* of all business effort in the United Kingdom today (or any advanced country) is put into providing services.

1.2 The variety of businesses

All businesses perform in very different ways and at very different levels. Your first thought when you hear the word business is likely to be 'a firm that has managers, workers, makes lots of money and makes a profit'. It will probably also 'produce something'. The purpose of a business will probably depend on its size; for example, a corner shop owned by one person and a multinational supplier of computers have very different customers.

Businesses can be divided into three sectors.

Private sector   These businesses are driven by the profit motive, to make money in order for people to be better off or to make the business better off, and to provide goods and services.

Public sector   These businesses have the purpose of providing mostly essential goods and services for the community of the country.

Voluntary sector   These businesses are driven by the need to care for parts of the community at home and abroad by providing goods and services.

Let's take a look at the variety of businesses that exist within these sectors.

Private sector

- Sole trader
- Partnership
- Private limited company
- Public limited company
- Franchise
- 'Privatised national'
- Co-operative (profit-making)

Public sector

- Central government
- Local government
- Public corporations
- 'Nationalised'

Voluntary sector

- Charities
- Co-operatives (non profit-making)

Note that a **public company** is a *private* sector company – a rare bit of confusion. These types of businesses need to be explained.

Types of business ownership

Sole trader

Individuals own the largest number of businesses. Some work alone, and some employ a few people. Over half of them provide services.

Advantages
- the owner has total control
- easy to begin
- requires little money
- the owner keeps any profit
- the owner gets great job satisfaction.

Disadvantages
- unlimited liability (the owner could lose personal possessions if the business fails)
- difficult to raise money
- all responsibility lies with the owner
- failure rate is high.

To get started, the sole trader needs skills, knowledge, the ability to work hard, and the nerve to take risks. Sole traders must be organised, and have personal attributes like keenness, patience and courage.

Examples

Your local

- butcher
- corner shop
- paper shop
- plumber
- electrician
- garage.

Partnership

Any number of people, from two to twenty, can form a partnership. This type of organisation is common to doctors, dentists and accountants. Any business run for profit by these people is legally a partnership.

Advantages	Disadvantages
- able to specialise - do not have total responsibility - more ideas - more money - can borrow money more easily.	- unlimited liability - risk of conflict (over share of profits, control of business, shared responsibilities, personal friction).

This can be a **start-up** business. Legally the **deed of partnership** sets out the rules. A **sleeping partner** contributes money and shares the profit/loss, but is not active in the running of the partnership.

Examples

Your local

- lawyer
- doctor
- dentist
- architect.

Private limited company

This type of business has **limited liability** which means that shareholders are only liable for debts equal to the value of their shares. This is a tremendous advantage in risk-taking, especially at the start of a business. Shareholders put money into the business and receive pieces of paper called **share certificates** in return. They then receive a share (**dividends**) of the profits. Directors and employees run the business. These kinds of businesses have Ltd or Limited after the company name and shares cannot be advertised for sale to the public. Friends and family often own the shares. The company exists as a separate body from the owners by law and therefore it could be declared bankrupt, while the shareholders (protected by the limited liability) could not.

Advantages

- the company is a **legal entity** separate from the owners
- it is easy to raise money
- there is limited liability
- the company carries on regardless of personnel changes.

Disadvantages

- complicated to set up – for example, legal documentation such as Companies Registration Office, Memorandum of Association (stating the main business activity and the amount of share capital), and Articles of Association (stating rules and procedures)
- audited accounts need to be made public.

This is less common as a start-up business.

Examples

Anything from local taxi firms and builders to big national businesses whose owners want to retain a controlling shareholding.

Public limited company

This type of company also has limited liability, and its shareholders can be anyone willing to pay the share price. It has **plc** after the company name and needs a minimum of £50,000 share capital. Shares are sold initially through specialist businesses such as banks, and stockbrokers and then through the Stock Exchange. Most shares are owned by institutions such as insurance companies, banks and pension funds.

This is very unlikely to be a start-up business.

Examples

Banks, petrol companies and companies listed on the Stock Exchange.

Franchise

A type of co-operation where a major established business gives its name and its product to a **franchisee** who pays the firm for the privilege of being allowed to sell its tried and tested product.

For advantages and disadvantages, see Unit 4.2.

This could be a start-up business.

Examples

Laundrettes, burger bars and mobile phone suppliers.

Co-operative

The most famous example is the Co-operative Group but most co-operatives are owned by all the workers in the business. Each worker has shares based on how much they contribute. Another famous kind of co-operative society is the John Lewis Partnership where all workers benefit from any profits made. In most co-operatives, all the workers are involved in decisions; there is no limit to the number of members.

Advantages

- members are always in control
- all members have an interest in making the business successful
- members share profits.

Disadvantages

- new workers need to buy shares
- often pressured to sell if successful
- needs new workers to expand.

Examples

The Co-op, John Lewis Partnership, Triumph and any firm that is closed down and bought by its employees (e.g. local joiner or a big car firm).

This is very unlikely to be a start-up business.

Central government

This business provides services to the public for nothing or for a fee. The National Health Service is available to all and is paid for by paying tax (income tax, VAT, National Insurance). Fees can be paid for prescriptions or dental charges, for example. There is a vast range of public services from defence to education to roads.

Advantages	Disadvantages
• shareholders have limited liability • easy to raise finance.	• expensive to set up • annual accounts and reports need to be made public.

Local government

Local government is run by local councils run this business, providing a large variety of vital services to everyone in the area. Services vary greatly; for example, fire, roads, libraries, police, social services and education. Funds for this come from central government, council tax and business taxes. This work can be done by the local council or **contracted out** to other businesses.

Advantages	Disadvantages
• in touch with local needs.	• can be politically driven.

Public corporations

This kind of business is rare. They are businesses set up by an act of Parliament and the government appoints a board of directors.

Examples

The BBC, the Post Office and the Bank of England.

Nationalised and privatised industries

In the past, the main features of the public sector were:

1. to provide the public with essential services
2. to prevent exploitation by private ownership
3. to protect key industries in the public interest.

In the late twentieth century, changes were made which meant that **nationalised**, i.e. publicly controlled, businesses such as coal, steel, gas, electricity, water, rail, communications, were sold to become private, profit-making businesses – in other words, they were **privatised**. This new arrangement has had major success on the profit-making front, but less success in providing good quality service throughout the public sector. These new plcs are still supervised by the Government to ensure 'fair play'. Local services such as canteens and building work can be contracted out to private firms by the local authority.

Example

In public transport, the privatisation of rail services and the takeover of Railtrack by the Government in 2001 is an example of the difficulties and conflicts faced by service providers.

The main advantages of public sector businesses are:

- They do not want to make a profit at all costs.
- They particularly want to help those who need help the most.
- They want to provide a service or product to the whole nation.
- They want to be better than the competition.

The main disadvantages of public sector businesses are:

- They search for a low-cost service and quality may suffer.
- They are monopolies and can become complacent.
- They may become inefficient due to slack management.
- They are dependent on the government for funding.

The main advantages of privatisation of public sector businesses are:

- The profit motive means more attention to consumer needs.
- They have more awareness of the market place.
- They have to compete for business.
- They are answerable to shareholders and their votes.

The main disadvantages of privatisation of public sector businesses are:

- The profit motive means higher prices and charges.
- Plcs may abuse the power they have in the marketplace.
- Once the contract is won, the businesses may take advantage of their position.
- Promises on quality of service may not be honoured.

Charities

These businesses provide a targeted service for special sections of the community – for instance, Shelter for the homeless and those with housing problems. While many charity employees are volunteers, the top managers are paid professionals. Finance can come from the National Lottery, public donations, business donations and government contributions.

Advantages

- flexible response to needs
- absolutely essential to the needs of a country.

Disadvantages

- run by volunteers, often not as a 'business'
- good intentions can overcome business sense.

Examples

Local hospices, Shelter, creches, Save the Children and Mind.

1.3 Types of production

From planting seeds in the ground to the extraordinary variety of food available in supermarkets and restaurants, our everyday lives depend on a chain of events known as production.

Primary production covers **raw materials** which are basic and straight from land, sea and air. Examples are mining, farming, fishing, forestry, quarrying, oil and gas. In some countries where there is very little natural water, water is extracted from the sea.

Primary production

Secondary production uses these raw materials to make finished goods. The range is vast – from a nail to a cruise liner, from a teabag to a 100-storey block of flats. Putting things together is part of this type of production and therefore building and the construction industry are included. The industries known as the **utilities** include water, gas and electricity.

Secondary production

Tertiary production covers all services and counts as the biggest sector by far. Tertiary production could be grouped under the following services: personal, commercial, transport, distribution, financial and the arts.

Tertiary production

1.4 The production chain

Everybody is a maker and a user, whether we are making a good or providing a service, or whether we are using water or electricity.

Production *or* operations

Production is the transformation of raw materials into a finished article offered for sale. Businesses use resources to make products. There are different methods of production but they do have many similarities. This is the key function of **operations** or the **production chain**.

This is basically what is described as **IPO** or **Input → Process → Output.**

Input = raw materials and parts; relies on good suppliers and good stock control.

Process = puts inputs together to make end product; relies on good people and reliable machinery.

Output = the end product; relies on supply of inputs and quality control of the process.

Production needs to be organised and controlled. This is **operations management**. For instance, inputs must be bought at the best price, and the business needs to make sure that the product or service is available at the right time.

Various businesses help to meet each others' needs when producing a product for the consumer. There is a high degree of interdependence among the organisations involved in the various stages of production. For example, if an early product or process is poor, then the final product will be poor. Problems can arise at any stage if the production process is weak or badly managed.

As we have noted already, there is a big difference between the production of goods (pencils, cameras and cruise liners) and the provision of services (banking, hotels, hairdressing and dentists). Services need inputs, including the obvious resource of people, to function. A dentist needs specialist equipment, at least six years at university, skilled assistants to x-ray, prepare and receive patients, computers for databases, a location, supplies and so on. A hockey team has a pitch, equipment, advertising and promotion, sponsors, the Hockey Union, volunteers, resources and, most of all, good players. What about your local hairdresser, leisure centre, hospital, taxi-driver, fashion shop and baker? They all supply a service and they will all go about it in different ways.

Product-led operations – Sometimes decisions on what to produce come from an invention or a new product. Consumers have not bought the item before and they purchase the good or service because of its expected quality or usefulness. This is termed **product-led**

operations. This kind of business can be quite uncertain, as the market has not been tested before.

Market-led operations – Much of the time, the market place is governed by the law of the consumer. What the consumer wants, the consumer gets – the customer is always right! This is often an easier way to run a business, since if you can find out what consumers want, you can produce it to their description. This is called **market-led operations**.

1.5 Money or wealth?

Did you know?

'Money makes the world go round', according to the singer in *Cabaret*, set in Germany in the 1930s. But Germany had a bad attack of **hyperinflation** (very severe inflation) in 1923 when a barrow-load of banknotes was needed to buy a loaf of bread.

What about wealth then? Wealth is *not* money! It can end up that way, but money is obtained by creating wealth. Here's how:

At each stage in any business, **value** is added to the **cost** or **price**. For instance, in the chain below, each part has a cost and a price.

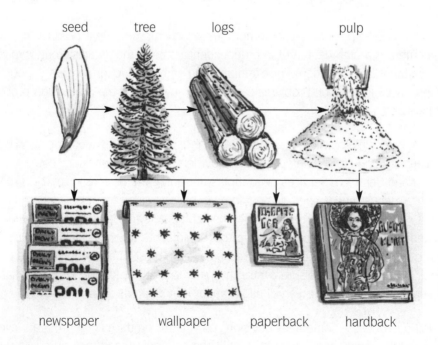

seed   tree   logs   pulp

newspaper   wallpaper   paperback   hardback

Stages of production

When all these parts are added together, you find the final **selling price** of the good to the customer. But each part has a special price for each customer at each stage. In other words, each stage or business takes its cut! This is sometimes called the **value added**.

Businesses try to satisfy all needs and wants – whether they are old, established ones (beds) or brand-new, invented ones (computers).

You will have worked out that, in each kind of process (primary, secondary and tertiary), people are employed, people own firms and people invest in firms. Each of these groups (**stakeholders**) will want some **return** (or wealth) – it might be money, it might be growth or it might be just reputation. Some return is needed for their investment or labour.

In today's competitive market, all firms must be as efficient as possible to ensure they meet their customers' aims and objectives and survive.

1.1 What you really, really want!

1 Name four needs we all have. Explain a 'need'.

2 Name four (very different) wants that we might have. Explain a 'want'.

3 Describe three types of good. Give an example of each.

4 Describe a service. Give five (very different) examples of a service.

1.2 The variety of businesses

1 Explain the word 'business'. Give a present-day example that sums up the word business for you.

2 Give the names of and describe the three main sectors of business. Give an example of each.

3 Define a sole trader. Give a present-day example of one. Give two advantages and two disadvantages of being a sole trader.

4 What three qualities does a sole trader need to get started?

5 Define a partnership. Give a local example. Give two advantages and two disadvantages of being in a partnership.

6 In business what is a sleeping partner?

7 Define a private limited company. How is it financed? Give a local example. Give two advantages and two disadvantages of a private limited company.

8 Define a public limited company. How is it financed? Give an example.

9 Explain a franchise. Give an example.

10 Explain a co-operative. Give two advantages and two disadvantages. Give an example.

11 Explain central government. Give one advantage and one disadvantage of a business run by central government.

12 Describe how central government raises money and how it spends it.

13 Explain local government. Give one advantage and one disadvantage of a business run by local government.

14 Describe how local government raises money and how it spends it.

15 Describe a public corporation.

16 Explain the term 'privatised'. Give two examples of businesses that have been privatised.

17 Give two advantages and two disadvantages of nationalising a business.

18 Give two advantages and two disadvantages of privatising a business.

19 Define a charity. Give one advantage and one disadvantage of a business run as a charity. Explain how it is financed.

1.3 Types of production

1. Define primary production. Give two examples.
2. Define secondary production. Give two examples.
3. Define tertiary production. Give two examples.

1.4 The production chain

1. Define the term 'operations'.
2. Describe the four stages of the production chain. Give an example of each stage.
3. What is IPO?
4. Name three inputs needed to produce any good of your choice.
5. Name three inputs needed to provide any service of your choice.
6. Explain product-led operations.
7. Explain market-led operations.

1.5 Money or wealth?

1. Describe the difference between money and wealth.
2. What is 'value added'?

Test your decision-making skills

1. Prepare a shopping list to show your top five wants.
2. Estimate the costs associated with each of these wants.
3. Use ICT to prepare a chart showing:

Basic Wants	Luxury Wants

4. Complete the following table to show which items are goods and which are services:

	Good	Service
Football match		
Police		
Mars bar		
Hat		
Sky TV		
Internet service provider		

⑤ Prepare a table to show lists of durable and non-durable goods.

⑥ Match the following objectives to a type of business organisation. Your choice is private, public or voluntary.

  a I want to be *the* most successful person on this planet who sells shoes!

  c I want to raise funds to help those in need!

  d I want to offer the best possible service to local communities in the UK; after all, hard-earned tax pays for it!

⑦ Based on your local community, find out details about a sole trader, partnership, plc or charity. On the basis of your findings prepare a presentation using one of the following options:

  a presentation

  b handout

  c electronic presentation.

⑧ Match the description of the stages in a production cycle. Remember your choice is primary, secondary, or tertiary.

  a transformation of raw materials to finished products

  b offer of goods/services to the public

  c obtain raw materials.

Why do businesses exist?

In this unit you will learn about:

- enterprise, entrepreneurship and risk-taking
- profit, charity and public service
- the aims of different types of organisations
- stakeholders
- social costs and benefits
- economic costs and benefits.

2.1 / The purpose of business

As you saw in Unit 1, there are many kinds of business. They exist for a wide variety of reasons. The main – but not the only – reasons for a business existing might be:

- to provide a service (like a school)
- for charitable purposes (like Comic Relief)
- to make a profit (from sole trader to multi-national)
- to develop a good idea (any entrepreneur).

Providing a service

This is the biggest part of our active lives in the UK. About two-thirds of the population work to provide a service to customers – from a carry-out to a hospital. A good service can help to improve your standard of living. Funding can be public or private.

Charities

Charities are often supported by volunteers, but they can also be run as a business. The overall aim is to provide help for those who need it – for example, cancer victims, care homes for the elderly, foreign aid for famine or flood victims, and environmental activity against nuclear pollution. There are hundreds of these businesses and they are supported by thousands of volunteers. Funding is usually by donation.

Making money

Making money, many people believe, is the sole reason for starting or running a business. Any business plan of a sole trader, partnership, private limited company (Ltd) or a public limited company (plc) will focus on the target of making a certain amount of profit to pay the bills, to 'plough back' into the business, to pay the shareholders and to pay bonuses. Funding is usually by investment from shareholders and loans.

Enterprise

It is no coincidence that the Star Trek spaceship which 'boldly goes where no-one has gone before' is called the 'Enterprise'. That's exactly what an enterprise is about – the intrepid **entrepreneur** ventures into the unknown, makes a connection no one has made before, and uses resources in an original way. Who would have thought of gluing a pan scrubber and sponge together! A genius? You will find **enterprise** in many kinds of business – see a chance, take it, make it work, stick with it and retire happy.

You have to ask!

When your business starts up and begins to develop, you should ask yourself these questions:

- Will I fail (+/-)?
- Can I do it (self-awareness)?
- Have I the skills (human resources, job specification [see Unit 10])?
- Have I the qualities needed (human resources, person specification)?
- Will the idea work (market research)?
- Can I manage (operations)?
- What about the money (finance)?

You are calculating the **risks** involved in running an enterprise. Since even crossing the road is a risk, the idea of taking risks will not be new to you. It is the proper calculating of the level of risk that may separate the good business from the struggling one.

This means that you weigh up the factors or influences on your decision and then take a course of action – whether it is to cross the road, produce 100,000 new cars, or provide a new home delivery service.

What's available to support you?

You will need to use all the functions of the business available to you – human resources, finance, operations and market research. The effects of your decisions on a business might be listed as:

- the effect on the market
- the effect on the other products
- the costs involved
- the training needed
- the effect on jobs.

There is usually a 'spark' or a catalyst that causes a business to start up. This is usually some form of enterprise – the ability or vision to make connections, to have an idea, to take a risk. If you are an **entrepreneur**, the reasons for being a risk-taker might be as follows:

- to survive
- to grow
- to make big profits
- to grab a bigger market share
- to improve conditions
- to be efficient
- to lead the field
- to ensure quality
- to be lucky – being in the right place at the right time. .

Examples

Kwikfit, Virgin, easyJet, McDonald's, DX Communications.

2.3   Targets and goals

The main purpose of a business may change from one week to the next, depending on its success or failure. Some of these 'goals' are given below.

Private sector – the profit-maker

- to survive
- to break even
- to maximise profits
- to increase owner's/shareholders' returns
- to expand the product/service range
- to expand the business
- to improve the quality of the product/service.

Charity – the aid provider

- to help people (e.g. hospices)
- to maximise cash collection (e.g. street collections)
- to offer community services (e.g. meals on wheels)
- to recruit more helpers
- to open more branches/shops
- to widen the scope of assistance (e.g. partnership with sports clubs).

Public sector – the service provider

- to improve the quality of service
- to cut costs/break even
- to raise revenue (e.g. hospital trusts).

2.4 Stakeholders

This has nothing to do with vampires! It is a business term for groups of people who have an interest in how your business progresses.

Imagine a new 'soap' is being created for television. Who would benefit if it could attract twenty million viewers? The list would include the television company, the costume makers, the set designers, the caterers, the scriptwriters, the lighting engineers, the casting directors and, of course, the actors. They all have an interest in this soap going on and on and on. In other words they have a **stake** in the future success of the enterprise.

You could easily name ten **stakeholders** in your school – parents, pupils, school governors, pupil council, the office, the teachers, the janitors, the cleaners, the canteen, the window cleaners, the local council – oops, that's eleven. See how easy it is.

The main groups of people involved in business activity are:

- owners
- managers
- employees
- shareholders
- customers
- government (collecting taxes from the business).

Owners put their own money into a business. Managers are employed by owners to oversee the day-to-day running of the business. Employees are paid to work for the business and shareholders own shares in the business. Customers buy the goods and services produced, and the government wants the business to succeed to provide wealth for the country. (See Unit 8 for more on stakeholders.)

Let's take a look at the effects of decision-making on people and the communities they live in.

American electronics giant Cyborg to locate in Machrihanish

What a headline! The local people in this quiet village in rural Argyll would be delighted to hear of this big boost to the area, wouldn't they? Or would they?

It becomes a matter of balancing the bad points with the good points, the **costs** and the **benefits**. Its world-famous golf course might have its wonderful views of the Atlantic rollers spoiled, but it will gain lots of new members.

Local natural resources will be affected (e.g. farmers and wildlife), but the local **infrastructure** (e.g. roads, sewage, lighting, electric power, transport and so on) will be improved at no extra cost. Local retailers will benefit from new customers, but they might have to supply new-fangled products or services. The local town might become jam-packed with traffic, and house prices may rise so high that local residents will not be able to afford them. Since the new firm is a global business, it may not use local businesses to build and supply its growth. The local councillors will not have an easy time trying to balance the good news with the bad.

In management terms, there is sometimes a need to consider the **social costs** and **benefits** and the **economic costs** and **benefits** if the business is to succeed.

Social costs

These are the bad or negative effects a business has on the community. They might be:

- environmental damage – air/noise/water pollution
- traffic congestion
- lifestyle change
- local services unable to cope.

Social benefits

These are the good or positive effects a business has on the local community. They might be:

- happier customers
- creation of jobs by the business
- big contribution to the local community
- creation of jobs within other local businesses.

Economic costs

The penalties the area has to pay for making a certain business choice are economic costs. It is a bit like a game of forfeits. The cost of what you do is what you give up. The cost of going out at night is the valuable studying you could do instead! In each of these examples, the economic cost is the one you don't choose:

- electronics giant v NATO base
- hospital v leisure centre
- shopping centre v new by-pass
- packet of crisps v bar of chocolate.

Where the costs may be roughly the same, the choice is made on economic grounds. Does the area and its inhabitants benefit from this business? Does it gain in amenity (usefulness) and quality of life? The decisions are not about money, but about the long-term value of the changes to the area.

Economic benefits

These might be easier to understand. They could be:

- people employed
- wages received
- standard of living up
- boost to local firms.

Other influences

Not only do businesses have to weigh up the social costs and benefits and the economic costs and benefits, but they also have to battle a growing presence – **public opinion** or activists. These interested parties try to influence the decisions of businesses by taking action that prevents developments taking place.

2.1 The purpose of business

❶ Give three reasons for a business's existence.

❷ What proportion of the UK's workforce provides services?

❸ Explain why a charity is real business.

❹ Give the main reason for businesses to exist.

❺ Describe enterprise. Give a present-day example of enterprise.

❻ List three questions to ask yourself when thinking of starting a business.

❼ List three effects your business decisions might have.

2.2 Taking risks

❶ Describe four 'sparks' that might make a business start-up happen.

2.3 Targets and goals

❶ Give five targets of the private sector.

❷ Give three targets of a charity.

❸ Give two targets of the public sector.

2.4 Stakeholders

❶ Define a stakeholder. Give four main types of stakeholder.

❷ Choose any 'business' you like and list five stakeholders in it.

2.5 Balancing costs and benefits

❶ Define a social cost. Give two examples of a social cost when a business locates in your area.

❷ Define a social benefit. Give two examples of a social benefit when a business locates in your area.

❸ Define economic costs. Explain by giving an example.

❹ Define economic benefits. Give two examples.

❺ 'Public opinion has no effect on a business's decisions.' Discuss.

1. Prepare a presentation containing the following information on a company of your choice:

   - company name
   - ownership details
   - objectives of the company
   - how the company started

2. As Chief Executive of a hospital, outline three possible key targets for the organisation.

3. As the new Managing Director of 'Supa Shoes', outline three possible key targets for the business.

4. As the new Director in charge of your Local Authority Housing Department, outline three possible key targets for the department.

5. Your business – Classy Communications – advises clients on all issues relating to communication. The Headteacher of your local primary school asks you to brief her on possible stakeholders in the school. Prepare and present the information.

6.

Mobile phone company offer "an insult" to workers

Workers at the troubled Easytalk factory in Fife are being offered free mobile phones as part of their redundancy package.

What are the economic costs of this plant closure?
What social costs may result from the decision to close the factory?

7.

Plans for giant chemical plant to expand in West Lothian

Up to 1000 new jobs will be created as part of the proposed expansion.

Weigh up the costs and benefits to the local community if the proposed expansion goes ahead.

How are businesses organised?

In this unit you will learn about:

- different organisational structures
- the size of the structure
- five functional areas – marketing, human resources, operations, finance and administration
- line relationships
- span of control
- functional relationships
- the difference between authority and responsibility.

3.1 Communication in business

All businesses have the same communication needs. They need to be organised to achieve what they have set out to do. They need to pass on messages and decisions as quickly and simply as possible. People need to feel they are working together in a 'fair' set-up. They need work to be done as well as possible in the most efficient way possible . . . and so on!

One of the most difficult parts of working in any business is passing on messages, instructions and information clearly and briefly. (The telephone can be one of the worst culprits in this area. If you want to find a long-winded and 'waffly' way of sending a message, use the phone.)

Did you know?

If you have not heard of 'Chinese whispers', it is where a message becomes 'mangled' and ends up saying something very different when it reaches its destination. A classic example from last century is 'Send reinforcements, I'm going to advance!' – a message from a World War I General to his army which was close by. The puzzled Captain receiving it (in the midst of horrific death and destruction) had to deal with 'Send three and fourpence, I'm going to a dance!' This happened because the message passed through too many people, possibly not in direct contact (a bad line!).

Having the right structure so that communications can be clear is very important. A **simple structure** would be a boss and a worker, as follows:

Simple communication

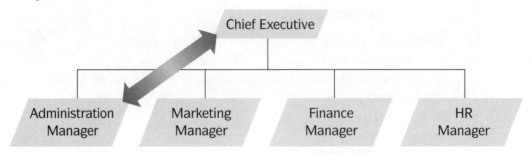

The advantages of a simple structure are clear communications and regular consultation. The disadvantages are that the worker is a 'jack of all trades', and under constant 'appraisal' by the boss.

In a more **complex communication** structure, there are several stages of command.

Complex communication

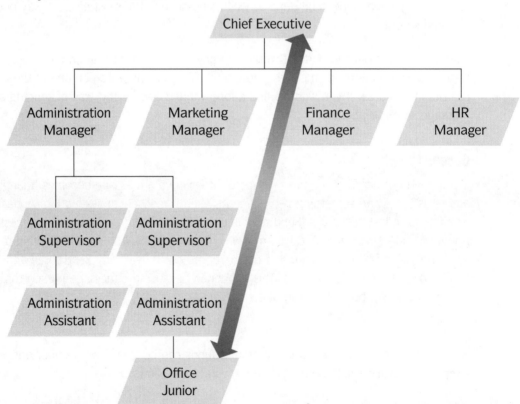

The advantages of a complex structure are that there are clear levels of responsibility and managers can monitor their subordinates more easily. The disadvantages are that decisions have to pass through several layers of management and junior staff may feel more remote and under-valued.

Bigger organisations, even with as few as ten people, can be organised in very different ways, or **hierarchies**. These organisations are referred to as tall or flat organisations.

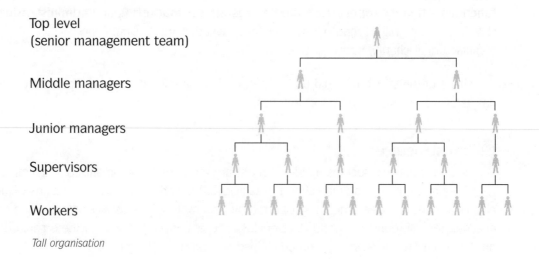

Top level
(senior management team)

Middle managers

Junior managers

Supervisors

Workers

Tall organisation

A **tall organisation** has many levels of management and managers have a narrow span of control.

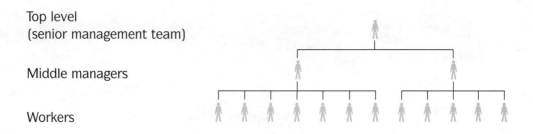

Top level
(senior management team)

Middle managers

Workers

Flat organisation

A **flat organisation** has few levels of management and managers have a wider span of control.

If you were in a business writing games software, would there be any structure? Would each writer just do his or her own thing? Is there a need for an organisational structure at all?

In a charity supplying clothes to the needy, does there need to be any organisation since all the workers are volunteers? In an airline, are pilots more important than booking clerks or the Internet site manager – and where do they all fit into the structure?

Size matters and so does the structure

What this means is that the bigger the business, the more the jobs have to be divided up. These are all the jobs that a sole trader has to do him/herself. They are divided into **functions – finance**, **operations**, **human resources**, **marketing** and **administration**. How this is done will depend on many factors – whether the business is retail, manufacturing, charity, public service, etc..

The shape of the structure could be tall, flat, circular, or even criss-cross. Each structure has its own advantages and disadvantages.

Global structures

Very large companies, such as multi-nationals, are too large to be organised in a simple way. They might be run by marketing forces across the world, but all five functions will be equally important locally. They might be run by geographically – distinct divisions and have headquarters all round the world (McDonalds for example), or they might be organised by product (Unilever for example) and be divided into product divisions.

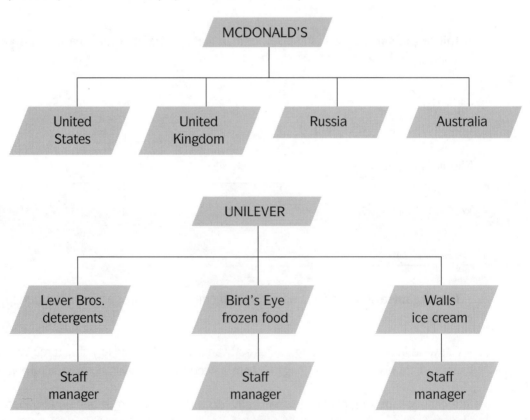

The decision-making process can vary depending on the way a business is organised. In some businesses, major decisions are taken by head office – this is called **centralisation**. **Decentralisation** is when decisions are delegated to regional managers which means that changes can be implemented quickly in their area. Some businesses may employ **staff managers** who do not fit into the functional structure but advise and support all departments.

The control keys – marketing, operations, human resources, finance and administration

Imagine an engine in a car. There are some functions in the engine that make it work – a cog will go round, a lever will move smoothly, power will be provided by fuel – and something will make all these functions work together.

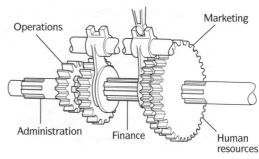

The word that we need to understand is function, i.e. an essential working part.

Every business has to have 'functional' areas and they are called:

- marketing
- operations
- human resources
- finance
- administration.

There could be a lot of argument about which is the 'fuel' and which organises the other functions. But the fact is that they all need to fit and work together to achieve the targets of the business.

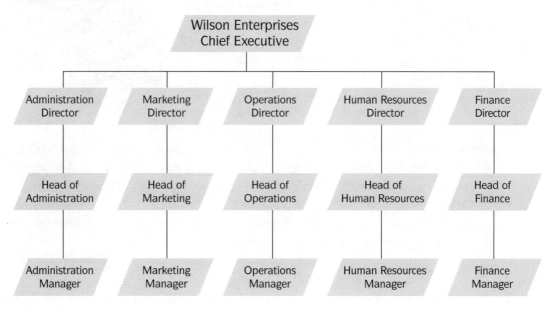

A functional organisation chart

Marketing

Marketing covers all the ways in which the business makes sure that its product (good or service) is what people want to buy.

Some people nowadays believe that marketing is *all* that matters in a business. It is only one of the functions that have been mentioned, but it is an important part of the business because, obviously, if you can't sell your product, you're sunk!

These are some of the main tasks in which the marketing department is involved (a main part of the **marketing mix** or a function is in brackets after each point). The marketing mix, which you will read about later, is known as the four Ps – Price, Product, Promotion and Place. You know about the functions already.

- Carrying out market research to find out customer needs and wants (marketing).
- Trying to predict future buying trends (finance).
- Being responsible for advertising, packaging and sales promotion (promotion).
- Producing a product that meets customer needs and wants (operations).
- Calculating the price that meets customer demand (price).
- Producing the right quantities to supply customer demand (operations).
- Promoting the new product to the customer (marketing).
- Distributing the product to the right place, so that it is convenient for the customer to buy it (place).
- Providing an efficient service to the consumer and dealing with consumer complaints (public relations).

If a business decides on the correct combination, the sky's the limit!

Did you know?

There is a big difference between promotion and advertising; they are not the same thing, as you will find out in Unit 14. Advertising is only a part of promotion.

Always remember – no part of the 'engine' can work on its own. All departments must work together to make the business successful.

Operations

Operations covers the methods and procedures used to turn raw materials into an end product that can then be distributed and sold to consumers to meet their needs or wants.

- The operations department usually buys all goods for re-sale, and all supplies and equipment.
- It chooses suppliers.
- It operates strict quality controls.
- It organises distribution.

The main targets of any operations department are to produce the right product:

- in the correct quantities
- at the right price
- using the most efficient methods (lowest cost!); and
- guaranteeing a quality product.

Human resources

Human resources is the department which matches what the company owners want from their employees with what the employees want from their work (motivation, job 'satisfaction', and job improvement).

Its main responsibilities can be summed up as:

- looking after the employees
- recruitment and dismissal
- training.

These objectives can be met only through the good management of human resources or 'people and their skills'. In other words, companies need 'the right people in the right place at the right time'.

The human resources department needs to consider the following questions on a continuous basis:

1. What do employees want from their work?
2. How does human resource management help to meet the wishes of both employers and employees?

Procedures for recruitment

One role of the Human Resources Department is the recruitment of new staff. More will be covered in Unit 10, but the main procedures involved in recruitment are:

- job description
- person specification
- recruitment
- application process
- interview procedures
- induction training
- on- and off-the-job training
- termination of employment.

Finance

Finance is the department that maintains accurate records of all business transactions. Every business has to keep its finances in order, especially because it is accountable to stakeholders for the money going through its hands.

The main responsibilities of business finance can be summed up as:

- financial planning/forecasting
- cash flow and cash budget
- trading, profit and loss accounts
- costs and revenue
- breaking even
- assets and liabilities, balance sheet.

These headings will be covered in more detail in Unit 6.

Administration

In many businesses, a separate department or person is allocated to administer the business. The tasks usually consist of central, necessary, basic duties that are essential to any efficient business. These might be summarised as:

- keeping track of paperwork
- keeping track of any communications to and from the business
- keeping a record of any decision-making which takes place.

This can be done by organising:

- filing (paper files and databases)
- correspondence (word processing)
- messages and customer enquiries (phone, fax, e-mail)
- telephone and other communications
- diary
- small accounts (spreadsheets)
- meetings
- keeping records.

Much of this will be covered in Unit 18.

3.3 Roles in business

Let's focus on a well-known baker such as a Aulds or Greggs. Imagine the various kinds of people and relationships involved in that business.

People

Owners/shareholders make important decisions and are responsible for the employees, and for the effect the company has on the environment and on the health of their customers.

Managers follow policy made by owners/shareholders to get maximum efficiency and to protect the rights and safety of the employees. They must:

- motivate workers
- improve productivity
- ensure machinery/equipment and materials are used efficiently and waste kept to a minimum
- place quality checks
- ensure equal rights for all workers
- monitor spending by departments, set budgets and set financial targets.

Employees must fulfil their contracts and look after the health and safety of others.

Relationships

Delegation takes place when a manager gives responsibility and authority for performing tasks to people in less senior positions.

Accountability means a person is answerable to others for his/her actions.

Line relationships can be vertical (above and below) or horizontal (same level) and show the work relationships that business members have with each other.

Span of control indicates the number of people a manager has authority over – normally described as a wide or narrow span of control.

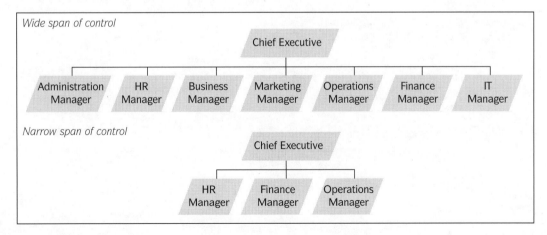

Functional relationships are about the different departments having links 'across normal lines' (e.g. Human Resources with Finance, Marketing with Operations).

Responsibility means a duty to carry out tasks and being able to make decisions that help to get things done.

Authority is being in charge and being responsible for decisions made in the business.

A hierarchy is a structure of layers of authority and responsibility with departments organised by function.

All of these ideas will be developed in Unit 17.

3.1 Communication in business

1. Name three needs all businesses have.
2. What is the most difficult part of business?
3. Give one advantage and one disadvantage of a simple structure.
4. Name the two basic shapes of organisations.
5. In a bigger business, what five functions need space in the structure?
6. In a global business, give two ways to organise the structure.

3.2 The control keys

1. Name the most important function. Give a reason for your answer.
2. Define marketing.
3. Give five of the main tasks of the marketing function.
4. What is the marketing mix?
5. Explain the difference between advertising and promotion.
6. Define operations.
7. Give three of the main tasks of the operations function.
8. Give four main targets of any operations department.
9. Define human resources.
10. Give the three main responsibilities of the human resources department.
11. What quote sums up what a company needs under the heading of human resources?
12. Name five procedures involved in the recruitment of staff.
13. Define finance.
14. Name four areas of business finance.
15. Define administration.
16. Give two main tasks of an administration department.
17. Name five areas of organisation in an administration department.

3.3 Roles in business

1. Describe the role of an owner/shareholder.
2. List four goals a manager has in any business.
3. What must an employee do in a business?
4. Explain delegation.
5. Describe a line relationship.
6. What is a span of control?
7. Define responsibility.
8. Describe authority.
9. Every organisation has a hierarchy. How would you describe a hierarchy?

❶ Using Cadbury's as an example, what functions will be part of their business structure? Helpful hint: try their website for information.

❷

Leading supermarket targets US online market

A leading supermarket is set to launch an online retailing operation in the United States.

Describe how a well-known supermarket's global structure may look.

❸ Using a local organisation as an example, design a table to show some activities of each functional area of the business:

Area	Activity	Example
Marketing		
Operations		
Finance		
Administration		
Human resources		

❹

Flycheap posts record profits

Low-cost airline Flycheap has reported record annual profits, with passenger numbers up 30% to 6.5m.

a Suggest four goals for Flycheap.

b Give an example of a line relationship within Flycheap.

c What is a span of control (nothing to do with wingspan!)?

d Describe a possible hierarchy for Flycheap.

Section 2

How do businesses develop and perform?

- How do businesses start?
- How do businesses grow?
- How do businesses survive?
- Why do businesses fail?
- What is a successful business?

/ # How do businesses start?

In this unit you will learn about:

- the need for enterprise
- taking, identifying and calculating risks
- identifying needs
- the market place and researching the market
- where to get money
- preparing a business plan
- external advice and information
- the factors of production.

4.1 / The entrepreneur

An entrepreneur is a person who successfully manages and develops a business enterprise using his or her personal skill, foresight and initiative.

An entrepreneur drives ideas forward and takes the risks that go with them, and they are often found 'swimming against the tide' to ensure success of a product. Early entrepreneurs were John D. Rockefeller and Henry Ford. Recent examples are Tom Hunter (Sports Division), Anita Roddick (Body Shop), Bill Gates (Microsoft), Tom Stevenson (Scottish Lighthouses), Tom Farmer (Kwikfit) and Richard Branson (Virgin).

Case study

Sir Richard Branson (born 1950) is the founder, chairman and owner of the Virgin Group which has more than 200 companies worldwide, employing over 25,000 people. Branson established a student magazine at the age of sixteen and founded Virgin as a mail order record retailer in 1970. The first album to be released on the Virgin record label sold more than five million copies. The Virgin Music Group continued to expand in the 1970s and 1980s and was eventually sold to Thorn EMI in a $1 billion deal in 1992.

Now the third most recognised brand in the UK, Virgin's interests include an airline, passenger trains, soft drinks, music, holidays, wines, mobile phones, cosmetics, record labels, publishing and TV production.

To draw attention to his business pursuits, Branson has been involved in a number of record-breaking activities. In 1986, he won the Blue Riband for the fastest crossing of the Atlantic Ocean in his boat Virgin Atlantic Challenger II. He has also broken records for the first balloon crossing of the Atlantic and the Pacific Ocean.

Name five people you know who 'fit the bill' as entrepreneurs .

The following are common reasons for people deciding to set up a business:

- to make money
- to generate wealth
- to provide a public service
- because they have an idea that needs to be developed
- to link up with others
- because they have good skills
- because they see a demand
- because they want a luxury lifestyle
- because they want to look after others
- because they can do better
- because they want to be remembered, e.g. Carnegie Hall (after Andrew Carnegie, multi-millionaire) and Aberdeen, South Dakota (founded by James McDonald born in Aberdeen).

4.2 Be innovative

Take a chance

> **Did you know?**
>
> The first sliced loaf of bread appeared in 1935 and only two years later, we had the pop-up toaster!

An innovator is a creative person who dreams up a product or service, takes the concept to supporting organisations (entrepreneurs) and then drives the concept towards the market.

The entrepreneur sees the potential success and profits, and funds the development of the product or service. By doing so, he or she takes a calculated risk – the entrepreneur will either receive rewards (in the form of profits) or bear losses (of money or personal possessions).

As all financial advertising reminds us, the value of your investment can fall as well as rise!

Extract from *Inventors World Magazine* (1996)

'Many of you will have seen actress Andrea Gordon on BBC1's 'Eureka!' programme with her sock-saver 'Little Feet'. This simple device overcomes a problem which seems to affect many people – the disappearance, or mis-matching, of socks in the wash. Although other people may claim to have had a similar idea, it is Andrea who, through a combination of a good idea, good design and a winning trade name, is set to corner this niche market.'

Crazy inventor – or thinker?

An inventor is often pictured as a crazy-looking, wild-haired scientist who spends all his time (it's never a her!) in the potting shed at the bottom of the garden. In fact, most of the inventors of our time are people who have little ideas that develop into historic discoveries.

The man who thought of sticking a scourer and a sponge together and then selling it as a washing-up device is now a multi-millionaire. And who would have thought that a wind-up radio would become world-famous?

Case study

Sir Clive Sinclair (born 1940) is one of the best-known contemporary British inventors. After first working for a technical publishing company, he has formed a succession of companies since the 1960s to research, develop and exploit the opportunities afforded by new technologies.

Sinclair first came to public prominence in the late 1970s and early 1980s with a succession of inventions based on the emerging solid-state electronics technology. His main achievement was to apply the new technology to produce novel products for the mass consumer. These included the first widely available pocket calculator, digital watches, pocket and wristwatch television sets, and a series of some of the first home computers.

His designs have not always met with a favourable reception, however. To the British public, he is as well known for his commercially disastrous Sinclair C5 vehicle as he is for all his successes.

What kind of business organisation would be best for a successful inventor like Sinclair?

This is a picture of Charles Babbage. What did he invent?

Answer: he is the man most commonly associated with creating the first computer. He was penniless when he died in 1871.

Franchise

Another form of business start-up is a franchise. Franchising is a form of co-operation in which one business (the franchisee) buys the right to sell the goods or services of another business (the franchiser).

A common reason for businesses starting up is in response to franchise opportunities. An example of such an opportunity is shown below. You are given basic information regarding the company and a contact number.

The type of franchise will determine the costs as well as decisions relating to location, staff and specialist skills required.

THE UK's NO. 1 PIZZA DELIVERY FRANCHISE

Do you want a piece of it? If so, phone (01234) 567890.

Setting up a franchise means both sides agreeing to a legal contract, which includes things like:

- the amount of capital to be invested
- the length of time the franchise will be in operation
- any support to be provided by the franchiser
- the royalties to be paid to the franchiser.

The advantages to the franchising company are that it can expand easily, reduce risks, receive regular payments, and get the benefit of ambitious franchisees. For franchisees there is a bigger chance of success, a more secure place in the market, virtually no cash-flow problems and continuous support from the franchiser.

The disadvantages for the franchising company are that it could find its name ruined by lower standards, it will have to bear initial costs and it will have to provide continual support. For franchisees the disadvantages are a lack of independence, having to make regular payments and not being able to benefit from success by selling the business.

Tycoon

What do you think a tycoon is? A person with loads of money? A very powerful figure? A very dynamic leader in business?

Jean Paul Getty (1892–1976) started business as an independent oil producer in the USA in 1914. From 1942–1961 Getty was president, general manager, and principal owner of the Minnehoma Financial Corp. From World War II until his death, Getty was one of the richest men in the world. The art collections he began to assemble in the 1930s formed the nucleus of the J. Paul Getty Museum, opened on his estate in Malibu, California, in 1974. Unusually well-endowed, it includes a library, an archive of photographs of art works, and conservation laboratories.

So what sets a tycoon apart from the average person? Success (usually achieved in business) – whether deserved or not – means that a person can accumulate a large store of money and use it to achieve an important ambition.

A tycoon's ambition might be to pay for the upkeep of all the major opera houses in the world, to keep a football team in business, to pay for National Parks to be maintained, or to build museums – and so on.

The Miami area in the United States was long inhabited by Native Americans. The first permanent non-Native American settlement was established in the 1870s near the site of United States Fort Dallas. Expansion began after the rail magnate **Henry M. Flagler** extended a railway to the site in 1896 and promoted the city as a resort area. St Augustine is a port and a commercial and distribution centre for the surrounding agricultural region and a popular year-round resort. Major products include transport equipment, clothing and processed foods. The city is the site of Flagler College (established in 1963).

Name three tycoons of the present day and describe what they do.

4.3   Finding a gap in the market

Market research, personal opinion or insight can highlight a particular consumer need. The aim of the entrepreneur is to match this need and break new ground. This offers the chance to capture the market before competition starts or follows your lead – and the earlier the opportunity for developing a brand loyalty in your customers, the better!

Here's an example of how an everyday problem can spark an idea for a new product:

> Extract from *Inventors World Magazine* (1996)
>
> 'Here's a simple solution to a common problem constantly faced by dog owners. If you wish to temporarily secure your dog while shopping or attending to dozens of other chores, then the Limpet Dog Anchor could be a godsend. The Limpet is a sucker-cup which will allow you to secure your dog to any shiny, non-porous surface and is easily removed by squeezing in the right place.'

Rags to riches

Another area rich in opportunity is the field of the arts, and literature in particular. Your ladder to the top may be writing a book!

Case study

J. K. Rowling began her writing in a café in Edinburgh and had no idea of what was in store for her. The divorced, unemployed, single mother has been transformed into a multi-millionaire thanks to the success of her Harry Potter books for children.

The stories of the boy wizard have caught the imagination of children and adults alike and have been translated into 42 languages worldwide. In addition to the success of the books, the Hollywood film of 'Harry Potter and the Philosopher's Stone' has broken box office records for advance sales.

In what way is this a 'rags to riches' story?

Branching out

'I can do better than that.' Sometimes an employee with experience believes he or she could do something better than their manager. It could be that you have found that you have specialist skills, perhaps in growing plants, and that your future lies in going into the garden centre business.

Experienced staff who have been well trained and have a number of contacts in a particular field may decide to branch out on their own and set up their own business, often as a consultant. This is a good example of how partnerships can be formed, with the different partners specialising in different aspects of business activity. (See p. 5 for more on partnerships.)

A partnership, is a term applied to an association of two or more people who have agreed to combine their labour, property and skill, or some or all of them, for the purpose of engaging in lawful business and sharing profits and losses between them; in this definition the term *business* includes every trade, occupation and profession. The parties forming such an association are known as partners.

There have been lots of world-famous partnerships in the past. Here's an example of one:

Case study

Rolls-Royce, one of the most famous names in engineering, was founded in 1906 by Charles Rolls and Henry Royce. The Silver Ghost car model was designed and produced in 1906. In 1914 Royce designed the Eagle aircraft engine, used extensively in World War I. Royce also designed the Merlin engine, used in Spitfires and Hurricanes in World War II. Jet engines followed and became an important part of the company.

Find out the latest news about Rolls-Royce by visiting their website.

Did you know?

Marks & Spencer was formed in 1894 when Michael Marks, a Russian-born Polish refugee, formed a partnership with Tom Spencer, a former cashier for a wholesale company. The company began life as a market stall before Marks and Spencer opened more prestigious premises in Leeds in 1904.

Buyouts

This takes place when a group of managers, supported by investors, decides to take over an existing organisation, assuming control and responsibility for its future development.

A common reason leading to a buyout is to prevent the closure of a particular factory with the buyout team believing that it can take the company forward and thereby secure jobs for the majority of the workforce – or save jobs!

Management buys M & S supplier

'The UK's Coats Viyella has said its contract clothing division – a key Marks & Spencer supplier – is to be sold in a management buyout.

The textile company said it would receive £12m in cash for the business from Marplace – a company set up by the division's senior management for the purpose of the buyout.

It will additionally retain assets from the business worth £17m for disposal.

Coats, the world's largest sewing-thread maker, had in September said it would sell or shut the division in an attempt to "face economic truth".'

Source: BBC News Online (4 December 2000)

4.4 Business support

The money factor

Money becomes available in a number of ways, e.g. from a redundancy payout, inheritance, or even a lottery win!

An individual suddenly has the finance to set up their own business such as a taxi service or restaurant. But far too many new businesses do not make it, so help is needed.

Help and where to find it

A wide range of groups offer support to people starting up in business:

- The Prince's Trust
- local enterprise companies
- local government
- business start-up schemes
- support packages from commercial banks and other financial institutions.

Consult all possible sources before setting out – the more information you have, the more likely it is that good decisions will be made (see Unit 16).

The key to success

'If we fail to plan, we plan to fail!' So what is the key to success?

If a business is to achieve its goals and objectives, then plans must be set to make sure targets are met. You will need to prepare a **business plan**:

- when starting out in business for the first time
- to show potential investors (e.g. banks) that ideas have been well thought out
- when planning for expansion.

If you are keen to convince others where you are going, you must tell them how you are going to get there!

The idea is that most of the elements that need to be dealt with in your business are listed in some form. It does not need to be complicated, but people who may want to help you start your business will want to be convinced you know what you are doing.

Some basic headings to get you started are:

- business aims (targets)
- the personnel involved
- the product – good or service (the core of the business)
- operations (production)
- marketing
- location
- finance – costs and revenue
- finance – assets and liabilities.

It is common sense that you should know all these things before you start. It is just a matter of putting them into the right order – for you and for other interested people.

Interested people might be:

- potential investors
- managers
- supporters
- partners
- other stakeholders.

You need to understand the basics so that you can prepare a simple business plan yourself.

The beginnings of a business plan (or proposal)

- A simple business plan should attract the reader's attention.
- It should be kept to one page.
- It should contain all the vital information, which will include the proposal, the benefits of the proposal and the support needed for the proposal to progress.

Your first try could be like this:

The background	● what does the business do?
	● type of ownership
	● key customers and suppliers
	● turnover, profits, and staff
	● number of branches
	● business name and address
The personnel	● key people (names, qualifications, job titles, age, length of service, previous experience, organisation chart)
Business activity	● explain more about the product
	● how is it special compared with others?
	● how is it distributed?
The market	● the market for the good or service
	● the price of the good or service
	● who are the main competitors?
Trading summary	● cash-flow forecast
	● overheads
	● balance sheet
	● profit and loss account
The proposal	● what the business needs (including what is being put in by the business itself)
	● its assets and liabilities.

After this first attempt, you might be able to fill out a more detailed and professional business plan.

Business name	clear identification of your business
Company objectives	statements about what your company hopes to achieve
Location/premises	address/description of your shop/factory/office
Management/staff	details about key staff, their experience and roles
Description of product/service	details like unique selling points, quality focus, etc.
Equipment	describe equipment available or to be bought in the future
Marketing plans	how you intend to promote the good/service
Financial position/plans	final accounts, balance sheets, cash flow forecasts, break-even analysis
Production details	description of chosen methods, how the company operates
Future aims	where do you see your company being in three to five years?

4.6 Factors of production

The right mix

In order to produce a good or provide a service, a business needs lots of things. These can be put together under the heading **factors of production** which means 'all the things you need to provide a good or a service'. Remember a product can be a good or a service and a business can be public, private, a charity, or voluntary.

The factors of production are **land**, **labour**, **capital** and **enterprise**.

Land is the ground (or what's on or in the ground) you need.

Labour is the manpower and skill needed to produce goods and services.

Capital is money available, now or later, and what money can buy.

Enterprise is the 'cooking' – mixing the other three – and the risks taken.

If you run a business, you will have to consider *all* the factors. For instance, to produce a packet of crisps, you need:

land to grow potatoes and to build the factory

capital to buy tractors, machinery, peelers, slicers and packet makers

labour to skilfully create delicious, flavoured crisps, run the business and market them

enterprise to mix all the above parts into an effective business, which survives and hopefully prospers.

4.1 The entrepreneur

1. Name three characteristics (or attributes) an entrepreneur might have.
2. Name three kinds of job that someone in public service might do.
3. Give five common reasons for people deciding to set up a business.

4.2 Be innovative

1. What kind or person makes a successful innovator?
2. Give a description of an inventor – in business terms!
3. Name five famous inventions from the last fifty years.
4. Explain how a franchise operates.
5. Give two parts of a legal contract for a franchise.
6. List one advantage and one disadvantage of a franchise.
7. What sets a tycoon apart from the rest of us?

4.3 Finding a gap in the market

1. Name two important aspects of a gap in the market.
2. Give two examples of 'rags to riches' stories and explain why they happened.
3. List three reasons for branching out.
4. Give two reasons for buying out a business.

4.4 Business support

1. Name three ways that finance can become available to start a business.
2. List three types of organisation that can offer support to people starting a business.

4.5 The business plan

1. List two possible uses of a business plan.
2. Name five basic headings a business plan might have.
3. List three possible stakeholders in your business.
4. Give the six headings of a first business plan (or proposal).
5. List four of the sections in a professional business plan.

4.6 Factors of production

1. Name the four factors of production.
2. Explain each of the factors of production and give an example of each.

1. Give three examples of people or jobs devoted to public service.
2. Give three reasons of your own for setting up your own business.
3. Why were Andrea's 'little feet' so successful?
4. a What invention is Clive Sinclair most famous for?
   b How do you think the world would manage without digital watches – and why?
   c Name five other devices with digital time controls.
5. Find two franchises in your area.
6. What were the main attributes of the inventor of the Limpet Dog Anchor?
7. a Why do you think J. K. Rowling began writing?
   b How did she show enterprise during her early days?
   c Who might she consult to have a book published?
8. Find two recent examples of an employee branching out and two recent examples of company buyouts.
9. Give the four factors of production needed to supply:
   a a packet of coffee beans
   b a car
   c a dentist's partnership
   d a charity dealing with poverty
   e a local government housing department
   f a road building programme.

How do businesses grow?

In this unit you will learn about:

- expanding the business
- diversification
- takeovers and mergers
- horizontal and vertical integration
- research and development
- reasons for growth.

5.1 Expanding the business

When a business finds it has established its product, whether a good or a service, it will need to cope with the challenges of success. Its product will be in demand and a normal reaction is to grow – to expand – and to move into a new environment.

Growth can generally be **natural**, **planned**, or **geographic**. Natural growth is where it happens without any attempt to make it happen. Planned growth is where each stage is controlled and forecast in advance. Geographic growth is where the activity is changed from area to area, either adding to or diverting resources to achieve it.

Taking on growth

Decisions regarding growth will depend on whether the business can:

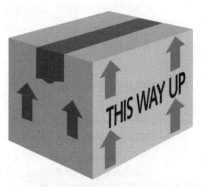

- make more versions of the product
- make a better product
- create a different image or packaging
- diversify (offer other types of product)
- afford the expansion
- increase turnover
- employ more people
- increase the amount of machinery
- increase assets
- increase profits
- increase the number of shares
- increase the value of shares
- merge with/take over another business.

Staying small

There are advantages in staying small.

- Management is easier.
- Workers feel they belong.
- Flexible working arrangements are easier.
- Finance is more directly under control.

Businesses may choose to stay small

- There are few union problems with staff.
- The community (through the workers) benefits.

Expanding **internally** means growing in size by putting profits back into the business. Internal growth often occurs as a result of an increase in demand for products. Businesses usually worry about planning this growth carefully, as it can result in disaster if not controlled.

5.2 / Widen your horizons

Dealing with challenges

Could you follow up the one good idea you had (and were successful with) with lots of other good ideas? Ask any business owner about this challenge and you'll find that it's one of the most frightening parts of the growth question. Constantly thinking of new ideas and making new inventions is one of the most difficult parts of any business. It would be much easier to take one good idea and have your business rely on it, its name and its offshoots.

It is possible for a business to have an excellent workforce, a product that is in great demand and *no* money to pay the wages and other bills – this is a problem of cash flow. On the other hand, the business can use its knowledge of the marketing mix to get everything right *except* that the actual price charged for the product is too high or too low. The result is no customers and a desperate 'last ditch' attempt to sell a dying product.

Diversify or die

Another way to advance is to build on the reputation of your product by diversifying. This involves developing new products or services for customers. This could be in the present market or in new markets. For example, a business could start as a record label and diversify into areas such as airlines, radio stations and fizzy drinks. Ridiculous idea isn't it?

5.3 / Takeovers and mergers

Let's do business together

What's involved in making the business grow **externally**? A **takeover** happens when a big company buys a smaller one.

A **merger** happens when two big companies combine together by agreement.

In business circles, these kinds of events can be described as **hostile**, **aggressive**, or **friendly**. Usually a takeover is forced on one of the businesses and a merger is agreed through consultation. They can take place when one of the businesses is struggling to keep going, but it can also be for very positive reasons.

The usual scenario is that the owners or board of directors will resist a takeover because they will lose control of the business, but will agree the dividing up of responsibilities and authority when it is a merger. Mergers are often carried through with a minimum of fuss.

Benefits of external growth

- The businesses grow more quickly by external expansion.
- There is no need to build a market.
- You don't need to find new customers.
- Your reputation is 'ready made'.
- You may even be gaining a quality product for no extra effort.

Conglomerate

A **conglomerate** is another way for the business to expand externally. It is a business that consists of a number of companies with nothing in common. It may have products that complement each other (e.g. bread and butter) and risks are spread over difficult market conditions. This kind of business expansion has to be considered very cautiously because it can expose a lack of knowledge in some of the products and a lack of experience in very different areas.

Integration

There are various kinds of integration – horizontal, vertical, lateral, forward and backward.

Horizontal – when businesses that make the same product join together (e.g. cars).

Vertical – when businesses in the same activity but at different stages in the process of production join together (e.g. fishermen and chip shops).

Forward – when a business at an early stage in the production chain joins a business at a later stage in the production chain (e.g. oil and medicine).

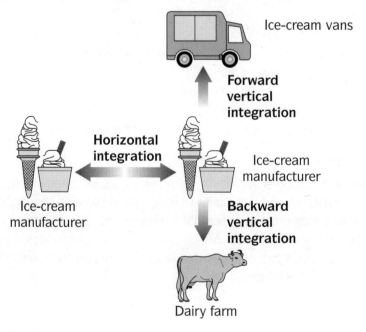

Ice-cream vans

Forward vertical integration

Horizontal integration

Ice-cream manufacturer

Ice-cream manufacturer

Backward vertical integration

Dairy farm

Backward – when a business at a later stage in the production chain joins a business at an earlier stage in the production chain (e.g. chip shop buys a fishing boat).

Lateral – when businesses that provide related types of product join together (e.g. ships and engines).

Some guidelines

1. Remember, growth can generally be natural, planned, or geographic.
2. Run your business properly and efficiently and it will grow naturally.
3. Plan your growth by deciding on a way forward, e.g. sell more shares, look for a higher turnover, and increase your market share.

Moving from the area in which the business began to a new location (whether it's still in the local geography or in Europe, or even further abroad) may be a way of increasing your business.

5.4 Staying ahead

Three main areas of business activity can help a business stay ahead of the competition: research and development, market research and product life cycle.

Research and development

Research and development (R and D) make it possible for a business to improve its products, make an 'image' impression on the public and create new products. It may also find new and better ways of producing the present products.

Did you know?

In the nineteenth century, the Bessemer converter transformed the iron and steel industry. The Luddites (who felt that the machinery would end their useful lives in the textile industry) smashed the machines up when they were introduced.

Technology is about how products are created. New technologies use engineering and science to find better ways of creating products. Businesses should be sure to keep up with new developments in technology.

Market research

This is a remarkable tool or function, available to any business that wishes to keep in touch with the customer's needs and wants (see Unit 14 for more detail).

Product life cycle

Knowledge of this will help the expanded business stay ahead of its competitors (see Unit 14 for more detail).

If a business decides to increase its size and influence, there are many good reasons for doing so. Savings that a new business can achieve on its own are called **internal economies of scale**.

Functions	Economies
Managerial	One firm needs one sales manager, but two firms may also only need one sales manager; this may mean more efficient management.
Financial	When you're bigger, it's easier to borrow money; you might even be offered better interest rates or repayment methods. A merged firm also saves on its overheads – e.g. one reception area.
Marketing	The marketing job can be carried out by one department; in fact a bigger firm might create one marketing department rather than pay outside experts to do their marketing.
Buying	Bigger firms can buy supplies at discounted rates – i.e. cheaper! Bulk purchasing means each unit is less costly.
Technical	Employees can specialise in their jobs; they become more efficient and better value.
Scale of production	When output becomes larger, the average cost per unit is reduced and each item is cheaper.

Advantages 'provided' by other people or organisations are called **external economies of scale**. They are often reasons to move to a new or different area.

Advantages	Economies
Roads/transport	Better roads and transport network (buses, trains, planes, boats).
Training	Better educational institutions and experts available in your particular line of business.
Labour	Skilled people who need little training – and perhaps there are plenty of them available (i.e. unemployed).
Local enterprise support	Specialist agencies exist to help certain areas of the country develop their goods and services industries.
Ancillary	These are the businesses that support your newly arrived firm – in electronics, supplying chips or websites, or in shipbuilding, supplying boilers or engines.
Reputation	Moving to a certain area may add value to your business – Silicon Valley, for instance.

These **economies** (or savings) reduce the cost of producing each item or service. It is generally thought that this only happens in the short or medium term (one to five years). Over longer periods, there are problems in growing bigger and these tend to push costs per unit up.

Problems of growth

Sometimes a business can grow too much and costs will rise. This is known as **diseconomies of scale**. This means that your business could actually become less efficient by getting bigger.

Internal diseconomies of scale

- poorer communications (too many levels or even too many jobs)
- less efficient/poorer quality control
- loss of business as customers get fed up with delays/bad communications
- the newly-merged business may not have a good reason to exist
- bigger wages bill and less control over spending
- employees lose interest.

External diseconomies of scale

- Congestion – the biggest market in the UK is London, so all businesses are attracted there. Traffic is now moving more slowly than it did when there were only horses and carts.
- Pollution – even if you ignore global warming, pollution (noise, air and water) would increase year by year, if laws are not passed to control it.
- Environmental damage – genetically modified crops, oil platforms disintegrating at sea and too much development are all examples of damage to the environment.
- Wasteful competition. One reason for 'nationalising' a business like water was to prevent wasting a huge amount of time and energy with ten firms all trying to provide the same thing – clean water. From the national point of view, there were a lot of wasted resources involved. Each firm would use people, pipes, reservoirs, dams and so on, so why not have one firm doing it all?

You need to have a good idea of the reasons for wanting to expand your business's size – whether by natural expansion, merger or takeover before you choose to grow it.

Motives for growth

Your motives for growth will include:

1. **Market control** – you want to decide what is produced (good or service).
2. **Market power** – you want to rule the world.
3. **Control of supplies** – it helps if you can be certain of your supply lines.
4. **Rationalisation** – this is where you are simplifying the structure of the market to suit your business.
5. **Internal economies of scale** – as seen above.
6. **Diversification** – where you spread the product range wider and provide more products.

Controls

The Government ensures that business life is fair and above board through legislation (laws). The main body (or **watchdog**) that controls some kinds of business growth is the Competition Commission. This body keeps a watchful eye on all types of business behaviour and acts like a kind of business police force. The Competition Commission replaced the Monopolies and Mergers Commission in 1999.

5.1 Expanding the business

❶ Name three kinds of business growth.

❷ List five decisions that need to be taken before you decide on growth.

❸ Describe three advantages of remaining small.

5.2 Widen your horizons

❶ Define internal expansion. Give an example.

❷ Name two of the biggest problems for any business.

❸ Explain 'diversify or die'. Give an example.

5.3 Takeovers and mergers

❶ Define external expansion.

❷ Define a takeover. Give an example.

❸ Define a merger. Give an example.

❹ List three adjectives that might describe a takeover or merger.

❺ Give three benefits of external growth.

❻ Define a conglomerate.

❼ Define the following types of integration and give an example of each:
  a horizontal
  b vertical
  c lateral
  d forward
  e backward

❽ Give two guidelines for a business considering growth.

5.4 Staying ahead

❶ Give two reasons for a business to carry out R and D.

❷ Give one advantage and one disadvantage of taking on new technology.

❸ What is market research?

❹ Give a reason for knowing about the product life cycle.

5.5 Reasons for growth

❶ Explain internal economies of scale.

❷ Give four of the headings under internal economies of scale and explain them.

❸ Explain external economies of scale.

④ Give three of the headings under external economies of scale and explain them.

⑤ Give another word for economies.

⑥ Define diseconomies of scale.

⑦ Give four internal diseconomies of scale and explain them.

⑧ Give two external diseconomies of scale and explain them.

⑨ Give four motives for wanting your business to grow.

⑩ Name the main body that make sure that business growth is 'fair'.

Test your decision-making skills

①

High street clothing store plans to expand its profits

Shares in Fab Clothing jump 12% as profits soar and more new stores are planned.

    a Describe the kind of growth about take place.
    b Why might Fab Clothing be planning to expand?
    c What factors might Fab Clothing consider when planning for growth?

②

Mobile phone recycling campaign launched

An innovative mobile phone recycling scheme is to be launched this autumn by a Scottish company.

    a Why is this business decision being described as innovative?
    b What will the company hope to achieve by this innovative move?
    c Prepare an advert for your local newspaper to promote this phone recycling business.
    d How could this company determine the size of its market?

③

ZX Insurance takeover of Alpha Cover announced

UK insurance company Alpha Cover has agreed to be taken over by ZX Insurance in a deal worth £300m.

    a What kind of growth is this?
    b What are the potential benefits for ZX Insurance?
    c What form of integration is being described? Give reasons for your answer.
    d What problems may develop as a result of this deal for customers and employees?

How do businesses survive?

In this unit you will learn about:

- the need to plan and control
- saleable goods and services
- costs, budgeting and cash flow
- using final accounts
- market research
- the trading account
- the balance sheet.

6.1 Plan and control

Every business begins with some objectives. One of these will be to make a profit. Then – after the excitement of creating a new business dies down – another may be trying to survive. Being independent will mean not having to rely on anyone else – but it also means counting on yourself. Planning is essential.

To be able to achieve the simplest of objectives, the business needs to plan and control. More importantly, it needs to plan ahead. It needs to have a **business plan**: it must plan its sales and profits, and the results of this activity. These plans must show **revenue** (money in) and **costs** (money out) since these will decide whether the business sinks or swims.

- It must know how much to produce in order to break even.
- It must ensure that there is enough cash to cover the bills.
- It must balance its accounts.
- It must work out its profit or loss.

There must be systems in place to help control the organisation's finances. The bigger the business, the more complex the finance will be. In smaller businesses, one simple accounting package on a computer can deal with most income and expenditure.

6.2 Saleable product

It goes without saying that every business that operates has some product (good or service) that it must be able to sell. Otherwise it wouldn't be in business. In the **private sector** (sole traders, partnerships, limited companies, public companies, franchises, co-ops), there is a central need for **profit** (**turnover** [total sales] less **running costs** [day-to-day expenses]). This means that suppliers can be paid, interest charges paid, employees paid, taxes paid and shareholders paid dividends. The drive for profits also encourages the business to keep itself efficient, with a view to possible expansion and investment, while staying aware of consumer demand.

In the **public sector** (government-managed companies and corporations), there is a central need to cover costs (or **break even**). Remember that the aim of the public sector is to provide the best service and not to make a profit. This can be done by the government setting targets to be achieved and deciding the amount of money to be used. Being left with unused money (or a surplus) at the end of the year is not good as it might mean the best service was not provided. Overspending might also be a sign of inefficiency. The best result of a public sector service would be to break even, where costs are covered by revenue.

Charities need to use as much of their revenue as possible in the service of their customers. As businesses, they pay wages, rent and other expenses and need to make very efficient use of their donated income.

Owner-run new businesses often have an unstated goal of profit maximisation, but larger companies or craft-based industries may have other aims such as quality or international influence.

A business must ensure it has an appropriate product and make sure the method of delivery is right.

6.3 Costs and cash

Every business needs to control costs. To do this, it needs to know and understand them as they affect the business. Meet Bill!

Types of cost

- *start-up costs* (some major expenditure to begin trading)
- *running costs* (paying for the day-to-day business of the company)
- *capital costs* (purchasing equipment or buildings)
- *fixed costs* (often called overheads, these don't vary whatever the production level), e.g. rent, rates, etc.
- *variable costs* (depend totally on the production level, e.g. electric power to machines, wages, etc.
- *semi-variable costs* (this is a complicated area: electricity can be split between the office and the production department – and there is also a quarterly charge which must be paid whether the business operates or not)
- *total costs* (fixed and variable added together)
- *overheads* (the name for fixed costs but can be used to include all costs)
- *cost of sales* (purchases plus any stock)

Types of spending

- *capital expenditure* – money spent on setting up the business; buying fixed assets (such as premises).
- *revenue expenditure* – money spent on running the business from day to day (such as wages).

Cash budget

Every business needs to set up and control its cash budget properly. A business will use the budget to plan for the year ahead. Every department will make its own budget and its forecasts will be carefully checked.

Human Resources, e.g. costs of recruitment

Marketing, e.g. costs of promotion

Finance, e.g. equipment needed to control costs

Operations, e.g. your factory extension

Budgetary control

This means that a business wants to feel that it is in control of its own destiny. It tries to do this by:

1. setting definite, short-term goals
2. putting down clear financial targets
3. assessing its business performance regularly.

Analysis of a cash budget

Costs may vary up or down – by the hour, the day, the week or the year – and these are investigated and controlled as necessary. The business needs to look carefully at the cash budget and take some action.

This could be to:

- cut costs – this is a favourite way to make better profits (too bad if the cost is your wages!)
- move to cheaper premises
- stop non-vital insurance and subscriptions, etc.
- do only essential repairs/maintenance (machinery v office – which suffers first?)
- reduce training programmes – easy to do but what about the future of your business?
- find cheaper materials
- cut advertising costs – do you need advertising?
- recruit no new staff – manage with the old ones, even if they're inefficient
- reduce part-timers' hours of work or introduce more part-timers (reduces cost of pensions, sickness benefits, holidays)
- cut expense accounts, company cars, etc..

Making major changes

A more direct but long-term way of reducing some overheads of the business could be to:

- reduce labour (cut the number of employees or management)
- increase capitalisation (replace people with machines)
- obtain cheaper suppliers (new businesses are always keen to impress)
- bulk buy (do not do this if you won't sell the product)
- share (the premises, the workforce, the office, the phone lines, etc.)
- outsource (use other experts to do the work for your business)
- subcontract (hand over sections of your business to outsiders and pay them to do it – like the canteen).

Warning!

The business must make sure any cuts or changes do not adversely affect the organisation's efficiency and its ability to carry out its normal, daily business. In other words, 'things mustn't get worse'.

Cash flow

Every business needs to control its cash flow – but first of all, what actually is cash? There are three easily described kinds and two more difficult ones.

Easy

1 **Cash in hand** is notes and coins; **liquid** means anything that can be turned into cash.
2 **Petty cash** is small sums in the office for immediate expenses such as milk and window-cleaning.
3 **Cash at bank** is money in a current account (bank or building society), which allows money to be withdrawn by cheque or debit card.

Hard

1 Other **liquid** funds include some deposit accounts where money can be withdrawn immediately.

2 **Non-liquid** assets:

nearly liquid such as investments (payment will be delayed), and funds in term deposit accounts (need notice)

less liquid such as **debtors** (people who owe you money), stock (finished goods or unused materials sold cheaply), and **work in progress** (partly finished goods sold cheaply)

fixed assets – can be sold at a loss (e.g. machinery).

Avoiding a crisis

The business needs to make sure it does not start a vicious circle of raising prices, resulting in lower sales, following this with increasing prices again, meaning lower profits. What does the business do next? Raise prices again?

If revenue is falling and costs are rising, this might mean bills can't be paid, because there is no actual cash – a **cash-flow crisis**. The business may have lots of orders and even lots of customers, but if there is no cash, it is sunk.

Crisis? What crisis?

If there is a cash-flow crisis, you don't need to be a genius to change things. There are some actions which can be taken:

- Increase your overdraft.
- Reschedule debts (have them paid in a different order and time period).
- Buy more on hire purchase.
- Limit the payment time for debtors (have them paying you sooner).
- Allow credit only on purchases over a certain limit (e.g. over £1,000).
- Increase your sales (e.g. by special offers, 2-for-1).
- Buy cheaper materials.
- Delay repairs.
- Reduce staff if no redundancy payment is needed.

What are final accounts?

Final accounts are a complete record of the business's finances. They give an up-to-date picture of the business's health. They are a good indication of what the future holds for the business.

A sole trader needs to pay taxes to the Inland Revenue and VAT to Customs and Excise. In both cases clear accounts are needed. Companies need to report to the Registrar of Companies and to their shareholders with their annual accounts.

Final accounts are prepared for the end of a financial period, usually a year. The business's work is divided up into three distinct phases.

The trading account

This summarises the basic work of the business – what money comes in from sales, what money is spent on purchases and what the stock value is at the start and finish of the year. This gives a figure for **gross profit** (or **loss**).

The profit and loss account

The gross profit of the business is the main income of this account, because it is mainly about the running expenses of the business. These expenses are often called **overheads** (such as rent, wages and insurance) and the total of the overheads is taken away from the gross profit to give a figure for **net profit**.

In some businesses, this net profit is used for paying shareholders and other items, but usually it is the final figure that shows whether the business can make a profit or **break even** (see below).

The balance sheet

The balance sheet is like a snapshot of the business, showing what the business has and what the business owes.

Any business has **assets** and **liabilities** – you have assets (like your computer) and liabilities (like owing somebody £5). They are given different slots in the balance sheet as follows:

fixed assets
current assets
current liabilities
net current assets *or* **working capital** *or* **current assets minus current liabilities**
capital and reserves

Expanding Enterprises plc
Balance Sheet as at 31 December 2001

	£ ('000)
Fixed assets	
Tangible assets	500
Investments	20
	520
Current assets	
Stocks	60
Debtors	20
Cash	100
	180
Current liabilities	
Creditors: amounts falling due within one year	(100)
Net current assets	
(Current assets – current liabilities)	80
Total assets less current liabilities	600
Long-term liabilities	
Creditors: amounts failing due after one year	(150)
Net assets	450
Capital and reserves	
Called up share capital	300
Share premium account	30
Other reserves	20
Profit and loss account	100
Capital employed	450

Break even

Analysis of the **break-even point** can be central to a business's health. It is a good safeguard against crisis.

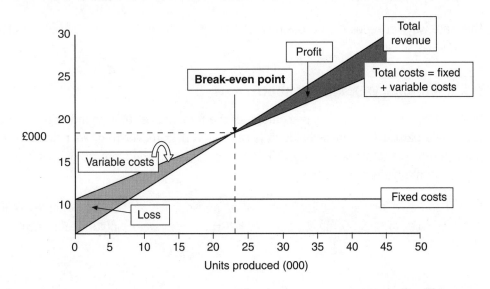

To plot the break-even point the business needs to know its fixed costs, variable costs and selling price (total or unit). The formula is **FC/(SP-VC)**.

This is only a projection (an educated guess) and doesn't allow for a rise in fixed costs, the difficulty in estimating variable costs, the possibility of the selling price changing, the sales pattern changing or stock remaining unsold.

6.5 / Market research

The art of knowing what customers want before they do!

The customers (or the market) must be satisfied. The following steps should be taken to ensure that the market is satisfied:

- The business must find out what customers want and how they want it delivered.
- The business must ensure it is an appropriate product.
- The business must ensure it is a saleable product.

Market research can be an instrument to turn potential disasters into helpful changes in direction for the business. If people don't see a need to help the starving in faraway places, can your voluntary business raise funds to help them in a new and exciting way? If your car manufacturing business produces a 'lemon', can you turn this problem into a new fashion item?

Examples

- The Skoda car changed from being a product which gave rise to many jokes (because it had many poor qualities), to being a product which is desirable to have for its high qualities.
- 'Live Aid' concerts created an atmosphere where it was exciting and fashionable to give to charity.
- Eating organic foods is not just 'sensible' but has become a new fashion.

There are ways of keeping your business at the top of the market place but also making sure it stays solvent.

Try to increase your market share

Market share is defined as the percentage of the total market that an individual product made by a particular business holds. It is calculated by turnover (e.g. your figure is 2,000) compared to the total market (e.g. 10,000): your share is therefore 20%. This is often measured internationally or globally.

Market share = company's total sales ÷ total market sales × 100; for example, total company sales of £25,000 in a market of £200,000 per week would give a calculation of:

$$\frac{25,000}{200,000} \times 100 = 12.5\%$$

Examples of comparative market share

National

UK soft drinks manufacturers – turnover in 2001:

Company	£m	Units (000)
Fizzy Bubbles Inc	450	56
Perfect Pops	380	32
Supa Drinx	72	10
Softee Sodas	15	2

International

Compare the turnover and profits of these international telecommunications companies.

Company	Turnover (£m)	Net profit (£m)
1 Tele ZX	750,000	65,000
2 Connect World	651,500	37,800
3 ABC Comms	325,000	29,000
4 Inter Exchange	200,000	25,000

Now that's what you call a profit!

Take a look at these financial figures for the international footwear industry in 2001.

Company	Turnover ($m)	Net profit ($m)
1 Dash	10,400	204
2 Concept Shoes	5,500	98
3 Go Faster	2,900	81

Just selling shoes seems like quite a money-making business – but how much are sales affected by fashion and how much high profile sponsorship makes for desirable products? It's a risky business – but if you can stay ahead, a profitable one.

Keep measuring for success

You can regularly compare your business with competitors in terms of:

- costs – wages, fuel
- profits – gross, net or after dividends
- assets – vehicles, stock, debtors
- borrowing – cheaper, longer-term
- number of employees – full-time, part-time

- stock market value – share price up or down in the last year?
- the quality of product – higher status, brand name.

Your business must keep doing this, even when it is doing well.

Size matters

The business must be careful not just to measure size, but also to evaluate its efficiency and its **productivity**. This is simply defined as the **cost of producing a unit per man-hour**. Many huge firms are inefficient compared to small firms because of their inflexible and high capacity operations. Just imagine how difficult it would be for a major car manufacturer to change its production line if a scare put people off any kind of 'people-carrier' or the colour blue.

A new product?

The decision to introduce a new product or service to try to 'save the day' might be counter-productive, because every last penny will be put into this 'unplanned' change of direction. Perhaps things have gone too far already or perhaps the business needs to make drastic cuts in various areas to save money, not spend more – although the decision to 'spend more to make more' can be a dangerous strategy.

For a full account of market research techniques and methods, see Unit 14.

6.6	**Financial information**

The information in the final accounts is like a collection of precious stones. If you know where to look and know your facts, you will be able to find little gems of information. The key to looking at the performance of the business is to use ratios that explore the financial data within the organisation.

With ratios, businesses can compare their own performance over a period of time and they can also compare themselves to other, similar businesses.

There are three areas that are analysed:

- Profitability – compare profits with sales, expenses and capital.
- Liquidity – look at the business's ability to pay its way (e.g. creditors).
- Return on investment – how much is paid back for the capital invested.

The trading account

If you compare the gross profit with the total value of sales in the year, you can work out how profitable your basic trading is. But what is a good figure? If you sell something for £10, what kind of profit would you expect to make – £1, £5? A very, very, efficient business might make 40% (percentages are usually used), which would mean £4. This comparison is called a **ratio**.

How much would a company selling trainers expect to make per sale of a £50 pair? How much gross profit would an oil company make in a year and what is its **turnover** (total sales)?

Three ratios from this account that you need to know are:

Gross profit margin =   *Gross profit/Sales × 100* (how much you are making per sale)
Stock turnover =   *Cost of sales/Average stock* (how often you replace your stock in a period of time e.g. supermarket v jewellery retailer – high v low turnover)
Average stock =   *(Stock at beginning + Stock at end)/2* (is too much money being wasted in keeping stock and how much is too much?)

Profit and loss account

As with the trading account, little gems of information can be found in the profit and loss account. For instance, how much of the year's gross profit is eaten up with telephone bills? Or is the company making itself bankrupt by paying far too much in wages?

The main ratio from this account is:

Net profit margin =   Net profit/Sales × 100

Balance sheet

In the balance sheet, the ratios become a little more abstract which means they are removed from the day-to-day business and try to look at the business in a more long-term way.

The ratios used are:

Current ratio   *Current assets/Current liabilities*
This is often referred to as working capital. It shows the amount of 'free' money the business has to plan for the future. A good working capital figure means the business does not need to have a bank loan to keep operational.
Acid test   *(Current assets LESS stocks)/Current liabilities*
Does the business have a healthy cash flow or does it not have enough money to pay its debts? Stock is removed from the calculation, as it may be difficult to change it into cash.
Capital employed   *Total assets LESS Current liabilities*
This shows how efficiently the capital is being used
Return on capital   *Net profit/Capital employed × 100*
This shows the owner or other investors what they are getting back on the money they have put into the business

Example

Use the figures below to give you practice in using all the ratios you have learnt.

Trading Account of Purley Pirates, video retailers, for year to 31 December (£)

Sales revenue		950,000
less Cost of sales		
Opening stock	155,000	
Purchases	530,000	
	685,000	
less Closing stock	185,000	500,000
Gross profit		450,000

(They had a net profit of £50,000 after deducting expenses of £400,000.)

Balance Sheet of Purley Pirates, video retailers, as at 31 December (£)

Fixed assets	Premises	120,000	
	Vehicles	40,000	
	Furniture and fittings	20,000	180,000
Current assets	Stock	185,000	
	Debtors	25,000	
	Cash at bank	2,000	
	Cash in hand	200,000	412,000
			592,000
Current liabilities	Creditors	50,000	67,000
Long-term liabilities	Mortgage	400,000	400,000
Owner's capital	Capital	75,000	
	Net profit	50,000	125,000
			592,000

6.1 Plan and control

1. Name three objectives a new business might have.
2. In one sentence, describe the purpose of a business plan.
3. Name three other financial needs of a business plan (an example is 'the need to know how much to produce to break even').

6.2 Saleable product

1. Define a profit in the private sector.
2. Define a surplus in the public sector.
3. Why must a charity have neither a profit nor a surplus?

6.3 Costs and cash

1. There are nine types of cost – name five of them and give an example of each.
2. Name the two types of spending.
3. Give two examples of a department's forecast cash budget.
4. State two ways a business can control its destiny through budgetary control.
5. After analysing its cash budget, a business can take ten types of action to improve it. Name five of these.
6. After analysing its cash budget, a business can make seven major changes to improve its performance. Name four of them.
7. Name three kinds of cash.
8. Give an example of liquid funds.
9. Give the three levels of non-liquid assets, and give an example of each.
10. There are nine actions which might help to avert a crisis. Name five of them.

6.4 Final accounts

1. Define final accounts.
2. Why are they called 'final' accounts?
3. To whom does a sole trader pay tax and VAT?
4. Describe the trading account and give two of its main items.
5. Describe the profit and loss account and give two of its main items.
6. Describe the balance sheet and give two main parts.
7. Define the break-even point.
8. Since the break-even point is a projection, name three results which are NOT allowed for in the figure.

6.5 Market research

❶ Define market research.

❷ Define market share.

❸ Name four regular comparisons your business can make with your competitors.

❹ Define productivity.

❺ Describe how large firms can be inefficient in relation to productivity.

❻ Why might introducing a new product be a bad idea?

❼ Give four internal diseconomies of scale and explain them.

6.6 The trading account

❶ Define a ratio.

❷ In the trading account, define the three ratios used.

❸ In the profit and loss account, define the main ratio used.

❹ In the balance sheet, define the four ratios used

Test your decision-making skills

❶ Using the table of figures below:
   a Calculate the gross profit ratio
   b Calculate the net profit ratio
   c Comment on the performance of the business based only on the figures.

	2000 (£000)	2001 (£000)
Sales	200	300
less Cost of sales	120	190
Gross profit	80	110
less Expenses	53	45
Net profit	27	65

● Using the table of figures below:
   a Calculate average stock for each year.
   b Calculate the rate of stock turnover for each year.
   c Comment on the performance of the business based only on these figures.

	2000 (£000)	2001 (£000)	2002 (£000)
Stock at beginning	200	300	400
Stock at end	300	400	100
Sales	20,000	15,000	30,000

3 The table below shows the trading and profit and loss accounts for the last three years of a jewellery retail business called Grabbit and Wrun.

	2000 (£000)	2001 (£000)	2002 (£000)
Sales	1,420	1,680	1,900
Stock at beginning	20	80	10
Purchases	620	690	800
Stock at end	80	10	40
Gross profit	700	900	1,050
Overheads	500	850	650
Net profit	200	50	400

a Calculate the average stock for each year.
b Calculate the stock turnover for each year.
c Calculate the gross profit ratio for each year.
d Calculate the net profit ratio for each year.
e Compare the performances of each of these ratios over the three years and comment on the progress (or otherwise) of the business (based only on the figures available).

4 Based on the figures from the following financial readout of the maritime business 'Fish R Us', calculate the following:

a Gross profit ratio
b Net profit ratio
c Return on capital employed
d Current ratio
e Acid test ratio
f Rate of stock turnover.

	2000 (£000)	2001 (£000)
Stock at beginning	18,500	25,250
Stock at end	25,250	22,500
Sales		
Cash	21,500	25,750
Credit	50,000	55,150
Purchases	56,750	53,750
Expenses	8,500	9,500
Cash in hand/at bank	3,000	4,000
Debtors	10,000	15,000
Creditors	18,750	20,340
Capital employed	50,000	55,000

⑤ Consider the following two sets of figures from the trading and profit and loss accounts of a small local business, 'Plimsoll Line', which sells deck shoes to yachtsmen/women. The owner needs help to interpret his results.

	2001 (£000)		2002 (£000)	
Sales		450		500
less Cost of sales				
Stock at beginning	50		60	
Purchases	280		320	
	330		380	
less Stock at end	60	270	70	310
Gross profit		180		190
less overheads		110		120
Net profit		70		70

   a Calculate the average stock.
   b Calculate the rate of stock turnover.
   c Calculate the gross profit ratio.
   d Calculate the net profit ratio.
   e Comment on the performance of the business, based only on these figures, and make some helpful suggestions about the future.

⑥ The following figures have been taken from the balance sheet of the public limited company 'Kitch' which sells hand-made cooking implements. All figures are in £m.

	2000		2001	
Fixed assets		100		120
Current assets				
Stock	40		50	
Debtors	50		50	
Cash	10	100	5	110
		200		230
less Current liabilities				
Creditors	50	50	70	70
		150		160
Capital and reserves				
Ordinary share capital		140		140
Reserves		10		20
Total capital and reserves		150		160

   a Calculate the current ratio.
   b Calculate the return on capital employed.
   c Calculate the acid test.
   d Compare the two years and comment on the business's performance.

1 Consider the following balance sheet of Wolf and Munch, a European electrical supplier.

	2000 (£000)		2001 (£000)		2002 (£000)	
Fixed assets						
Buildings	700		700		700	
Vehicles	20	720	15	715	10	710
Current assets						
Stock	80		10		40	
Debtors	100		60		110	
Cash	50	230	30	100	50	200
		950		815		910
less **Current liabilities**						
Overdraft	50		15		10	
Creditors	200	250	400	415	100	110
		700		400		800
less **Long-term liabilities**						
Mortgage	20		20		20	
Bank loan	30	50	30	50	20	40
Net assets employed		650		350		760
Owners' capital						
Capital		450		300		360
Profit		200		50		400
Total capital and reserves		650		350		760

a Calculate the current ratio.
b Calculate the acid test.
c Calculate the capital employed and the return on capital employed.
d Compare the three years and comment on the business's performance.

Why do businesses fail?

In this unit you will learn about:

- the business cycle
- cash-flow problems
- the role of the government
- poor resource management.

7.1 / Reasons for failure

After all your efforts, it's not nice to hear that your business is a failure!

As the manager, you need to face up to reality and see where things went wrong. There are as many reasons for failure as there are business failures, and there are hundreds of them a week – yes, a week! Therefore failure to make your business work is not unusual.

But why do businesses fail? Perhaps you were not prepared for:

- the amount of competition
- the level of advertising by others
- your competitors 'clubbing' together?

Examples of difficulties are easy to find in many areas of business:

Transport	Sinclair's C5, Triumph motor cycles
Farming	BSE health threat
Retailing	Marks & Spencer
Infrastructure	Channel Tunnel debts
Tourism	Terrorist attacks

Did you know?

Around 12% of Scottish businesses close within their first year, 25% are closed within two years, and around one third will have disappeared by the end of the third year.

Where these businesses have gone wrong might be difficult to explain, but using the four major functional areas (finance, human resources, marketing and operations) might be a start.

If your **market research** is faulty (bad survey, wrong questions, inappropriate sample of the market), the expected sales do not happen.

If your **operations** are badly organised (too much stock, wrong stock, wrong type of production), costs escalate and the product is too costly.

If your job and person specifications are wrong, recruitment of **human resources** will be badly and inefficiently carried out and you will have a poor, unmotivated workforce.

Lastly, if your **finance** is in a mess, the amount of money coming in and money going out will be out of your control: ultimately, you're out of business.

Very often, competitors who have been around longer, and who have more influence in the market place, can squeeze you out of the market by reducing prices, advertising more and promoting their product or service on a bigger scale.

This means that, just when you are trying to attract the attention of new customers, they are being distracted by new, improved offers from your older, established competitors.

7.2 / Moving with the times

Often, it is other people's actions which make life difficult for the business and not its own mistakes.

When more of the population is unemployed, less money is being spent and the cost of day-to-day living is going up, this is called a **recession**. If this is happening – and it happens in a sequence of stages or a **cycle** – then it is not a good time to find your business struggling.

The main method of riding out the bad times is to try to stay ahead of the market, to move with the times and to be aware of changing tastes and developments in the market.

One very influential factor over the last few years has been the third Industrial Revolution – the ICT (information and communication technology) revolution. Any business that did not welcome and adapt to this technological revolution (which has affected every business in the world) would find it very hard to compete. But if the business overdid the purchase of mobiles, palmtops, laptops, desktops and so on, it would probably bankrupt itself. The business needs to plan carefully.

Closely connected to a good business plan is the need to respond to change, but in a calculating way. Move with the times – cautiously. Of course this depends on the business. Any business dependent on the fashion world or working in ICT cannot afford to wait cautiously. It has to take chances or calculate the risks and hopefully move forward.

We all probably know areas of the country, or the world, which have become poorer because of changes in the economy. Over the last fifty years in the UK, the coal, steel and shipbuilding industries have more or less disappeared – and the making of 'British' cars has all but gone as well.

Many British industries have disappeared in the last fifty years

If you were a business dependent on any of those industries, from a local newsagent to a coal mine, to a supplier of engines for ships, it would not matter how brilliantly your business was run, you would have to close because of a lack of spending.

Most replacement businesses have been in the tertiary or service sector – where there was once a coal mine, there is now a heritage museum; where there was once a shipyard, there is now a marina.

7.3 / Financial failure

Failure most often comes under the heading of finance. The most common single reason is not being able to pay the wages and other bills. There may be lots of work on order with lots of customers calling up, but the need is for cash in hand or cash at bank to pay the bills. Without good financial planning, a business will fail.

A basic awareness of cash flow and of the simplest final accounts means the business can begin to see when things are going wrong. **Forecasting**, as it's called, is not too difficult.

The human resources department makes decisions on how many staff the business needs and how much it can afford to pay out. The marketing department has a budget that dictates the promotion campaign it can afford. An operations budget dictates how much technology can be bought, which location would be efficient or if expansion is possible.

Three main areas of finance to be dealt with are:

1 *Cash flow forecasting* – plan cash in and out to enable bill payment.
2 *Budget planning* – for departments and overall business.
3 *Accounting* – having final accounts to allow analysis and evaluation.

You have seen how to analyse the final accounts (Unit 6), how to evaluate using ratios (gross profit, net profit, return on capital employed), how to work out the break-even point in deciding prices, and how to predict profit and decide on financial needs. These should give clear warnings if the business is failing. Steps can be taken to change prices, staff numbers, wage levels, purchases, production levels, borrowing and so on. Even if it's not your fault, it should be possible to avert disaster.

7.4 / The business cycle

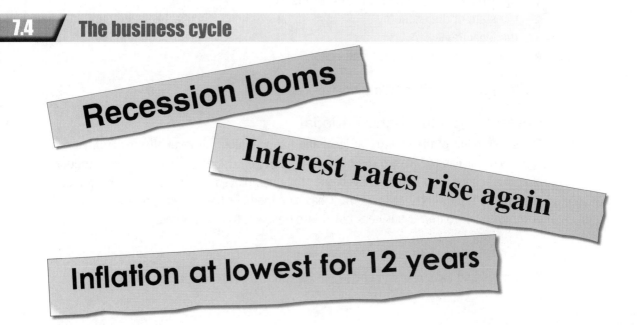

Recession looms

Interest rates rise again

Inflation at lowest for 12 years

Sometimes the business cycle is referred to as 'boom and bust' economics. This is when a period of prosperity is generally followed by a period of hardship. Whether it is bad management by governments or a natural order of life in the modern world, the cycle does exist. Over the past decades, there has been a regular cycle of rises and falls in economic activity (buying and selling), where business goes quiet and then improves again.

The solution (if you are in control) is to make the most of the good times and cut expenditure to a minimum during the bad times. There are businesses where this applies all the time – for example, seasonal businesses like fishing, farming and tourism. . .

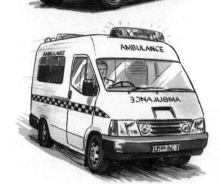

. . . and there are others where it rarely occurs.

The external influences (externalities)

Businesses – like people – are constantly affected by the environment, the conditions and surroundings in which they exist. People are influenced by their family, their friends and many other factors. Some of the main factors (more are mentioned later) that affect businesses are:

- changing tastes and beliefs of customers
- general social and political attitudes
- the strength and number of competitors
- the state of the economy
- the legal framework
- the government – attitude and action.

The last heading needs a little extra explanation.

Government – local and national

The government of the country at local and national (central) level affects all of us in many ways. It has to balance the need to encourage business against the need to look after the economy on behalf of everyone (the unemployed, the pensioned, the young, the consumers, the owners, and so on). It has to remember their needs and wants. The government encourages business but doesn't allow it to harm others.

Government – tax

The central and local government's greatest influence is through tax, for example:

- government spending (hospitals, defence, roads, etc.)
- direct taxation (income tax)
- indirect taxation (Value Added Tax (VAT))
- council tax (local council services – lighting, housing, roads, etc.).

Changes in the amount of tax taken or spent can have a huge effect on the country's businesses. Possible situations are:

- Central government increases its spending by 5% – a massive boost to the economy which means more employment, more spending and better services.
- An increase in direct taxation by 5% takes money out of people's pockets, so there is less spending, more unemployment and a lower standard of living – but only for those earning wages and salaries.
- An increase in indirect taxation takes money out of people's pockets whether they're working or not, giving the same results as direct taxation.
- An increase in council tax means that local government has more money to spend on local services like water, housing and roads.
- The interest you are charged for borrowing money is increased. This is set by the Bank of England (the UK's bank) because its 'bank rate' affects the rates other lenders charge. A drop in the rate will encourage people to spend more and take out bigger mortgages and will allow businesses with overdrafts and loans to have a little more money available for paying bills and buying supplies.
- An increase in the exchange rate (for exporters!). We're all Europeans, but any time sterling (our money) crosses our borders, it has to be changed into other currency. This applies to businesses just as much as to tourists. The exchange rate can rise and fall (usually depending on demand) and a commission (or interest) is charged on each transaction. A single currency in Europe would mean no exchange rate and no commission.

Restraints and controls

When a business is running smoothly, most of these restraints and controls will appear unimportant and insignificant. If, however, something happens to change any of the regulations, the business atmosphere changes with it. There are many organisations and laws of which every business has to be aware. Here are just some of them:

- Health and Safety at Work Act 1974
- British Standards – the kite mark
- Office of Fair Trading
- Competition Commission
- Regulators and watchdogs
- Sale and Supply of Goods Act 1994
- Trade Descriptions Act 1968/1972
- Consumer Protection Act 1987
- Trading Standards Institute
- Ombudsmen
- Local enterprise companies
- Regional assistance

- Data Protection Act 1998
- Equal Pay Act 1970
- Race Relations (Amendments) Act 2000
- Employment Relations Act 1999
- Sex Discrimination Act 1975
- Disability Rights Commission Act 1999
- Disability Discrimination Act 1995
- Human Rights Act 1998
- National Minimum Wage Act 1998

Surely that little list doesn't put you off running a business!

Poor resource management (or quality control)

It is very easy for a business to lose control of its resources, especially when it has entered the 'we've being going well for a couple of years now' comfort zone.

As you know, resources can be described as finance, production, people and the way they're put together (or **land**, **labour**, **capital** and **enterprise**). If the combination has gone wrong, the business will be inefficient and loss-making. Often the reason for this is easy to discover – bad planning or unrealistic expectations (usually found in the business plan which could also be badly out of date) are common factors.

Careful control of all the stages of production (**input, process** and **output**) would help to avoid problems.

- Don't pay for stock you don't need.
- Make sure the type of production is appropriate to the product.
- Don't produce goods or services that consumers don't want.
- Don't rush any part of the operation.
- Have some sort of quality control.
- Keep in touch with all employees (from management to the production line) to check how the business is progressing.
- Keep in touch with suppliers and have a 'partnership' type of relationship with them.

Whatever happens, don't panic!

7.1 Reasons for failure

1. Give three possible causes for business failure.
2. Give two present-day examples of business failure.
3. List two possible reasons for market research being the cause of business failure.
4. List three possible reasons for operations being the cause of business failure.
5. List two possible reasons for human resources being the cause of business failure.
6. List one possible reason for finance being the cause of business failure.
7. Describe two ways that competitors can influence your failure.

7.2 Moving with the times

1. Explain a recession.
2. Give two words that could describe a business's attitude to change.
3. Name two industries that have disappeared in the last fifty years.
4. In which sector are most replacement businesses? Give an example.

7.3 Financial failure

1. Name the functional area most likely to cause business failure.
2. State the three main areas of finance to be dealt with.

7.4 The business cycle

1. Describe the business cycle.
2. Name two industries that are often affected by this cycle.
3. Name two industries that are not often affected by this cycle.
4. Give three external influences on businesses during the cycle.
5. Describe the balance that the government needs to have in its day-to-day business.
6. Name two taxes paid to the government.
7. Describe what would happen if government increased its spending by 5%.
8. Describe what would happen if government increased indirect taxation.
9. Explain how the exchange rate affects exporters.
10. List three examples of legislation any business has to know.
11. Name the four resources any business uses.
12. Give the three stages of production.
13. Give three ways a business can control its production costs.

❶

Losses widen as APC Communications pins its hopes on Europe

Inverness-based APC Communications today announced pretax losses higher than expected, but it said it was optimistic after the first quarter showed "continued growth".

a Suggest possible reasons for a company reporting losses.
b If one company is making losses, others are making profits – what could a business do to turn losses into profits?
c Despite announcing losses, APC Communications is optimistic – suggest reasons for this.

❷

Bleak outlook for German businesses

Downbeat economic forecasts and disappointing company announcements paint a bleak picture for German businesses...

a What term describes this situation where an economy is struggling?
b What can you do to stay ahead in such an economic climate?
c What causes economies to 'struggle' from time to time?

What is a successful business?

In this unit you will learn about:

- achieving objectives
- keeping owners satisfied
- measuring success
- the different aims of public, private and voluntary businesses
- identifying the competing aims of stakeholders.

Achieve your goals

Some of the basic objectives of any business might be summarised as follows:

- to survive – especially if you're a new business
- to be independent
- to make a profit
- to increase sales
- to increase market share
- to provide customer satisfaction
- to be part of a community
- to provide a product/service
- to provide employment.

More advanced objectives might be:

- to grow year by year
- to be powerful – to have a say in the market place and beyond
- to have an instantly recognised product/service.

A **sole trader** may want to survive, make a profit, be independent and enjoy the work.

A **partnership** may want to share responsibilities and decision-making.

A **private limited company** may want a steady growth in profits and sales and more of the market.

A **public limited company** may want to satisfy shareholders, keep directors/managers motivated and satisfy employees in their working conditions and pay.

Remember there are many other types of business – charities, co-operatives, franchises and voluntary organisations – that will have slightly different goals.

A **charity** may want to provide more and more help to the needy.

A **co-operative** may want to save a dying business or provide employment for redundant workers.

A **franchise** may want to run efficiently within the parent company's guidelines.

A **voluntary organisation** (e.g. a golf club) may want to break even but provide a better service each year.

For every one of these businesses, success is measured by the goals set down at the beginning of each year, usually in a business plan.

Supergas plc

	£m
Turnover (Sales)	3,580
Annual costs	3,120
Net profit/(Loss)*	460

* (for retention and distribution and shareholders)

Burnside Hospital Trust

	£m
Revenues	250
Operating costs	258
Surplus/(Deficit)*	(8)

* (carried forward to next year's budget)

Auld Links Golf Club

	£000
Income	128
Expenditure	121
Surplus/(Deficit)*	7

* (for reinvestment by the Club)

8.2   Measuring success

In comparison, the measure of performance in a public service, charity or voluntary business can be a very complex and difficult exercise.

How do you measure the success of a charity? How successful is a school? In what way can success be measured? It is enough for the moment to recognise the difficulties and to see that stakeholders are central to the prosperity of a business. Some stakeholders might be:

- suppliers
- local community
- users/customers
- employees
- managers
- law and order.

Whoever they are, they all want your business to be successful and achieve their goals.

Different measures

Every business has plans and targets for its first and future years.

A **private sector** business (sole trader, partnership, private limited, public limited company) can measure its success by its ability to make a profit. This is simply turnover less operating costs.

Examples

Sole trader – local butcher, local greengrocer
Partnership – doctor, dentist, lawyer
Private limited company – taxi firm, builders
Public limited company – any firm listed on the Stock Exchange, such as Debenhams (national) and BP (multi-national)

A **public sector** organisation (central or local government-led businesses) is different – and more difficult to analyse. Since a profit is not expected, the judgement on success will be based on breaking even and on the quality of the service offered. There is also the need to meet strict financial targets to show efficiency and good use of public money.

Examples

National – defence, roads, education, health
Local – education, housing, lighting, sewage

A **voluntary** business (run mainly by volunteer workers) is a more complex challenge. It might even accept a loss as an encouraging sign if the aid offered (in giving people support, housing, food, medicine and other 'life-vital' products) has been supplied in a greater quantity. If there is a major emergency, like floods, famine, disease or war, then huge losses may be the result of its activity in monetary terms but those supplying the finance may accept these losses in the long term.

Some voluntary organisations are totally run by volunteers and some are run as international businesses. They provide a vast variety of support to the needy.

Examples

Amnesty International
Save the Children
Local hospices
Churches

Médicins sans Frontières
Red Cross
Oxfam
Imperial Cancer Research

Summing up, in the most common businesses (90% employ less than ten people), the target will be to make a profit. For the others, life is more complex with many different kinds of demands being made on the organisation.

Stakeholders

In any business, there are various people or groups (**stakeholders**) that require results which suit them.

The **owners** have invested their own money for the business to progress. They will obviously want a say in any decisions made and they require the business to generate profits.

The **managers** are employed by the business and sometimes have special arrangements where their pay is linked to its performance. These managers (or **directors**) look after the daily performance on behalf of the owners and shareholders.

(Sole traders are usually the owner *and* the manager. Most other businesses employ managers who have special skills in areas or functions like finance, marketing, operations or human resources.)

The **employees** have an interest in the progress of the business as they wish to remain employed and, more positively, to be part of a successful business.

The **shareholders** have an interest in how their shares are performing and therefore the performance of the business. There are two aspects – the price of the share on the stock market and the **dividend** paid on the shares.

Private limited company shareholders can be more supportive and flexible because they are usually employees, family or friends who have the long-term future of the business at heart.

Public limited company shareholders tend to be more detached from the business and look only at share prices (which can rise or fall for reasons unconnected to your business's performance) and dividends (which are usually closely linked to annual performance).

All the above have an easy measure of success – money.

Stakeholders want their piece of the action

One way of trying to explain a **stake** is to refer to a piece of fiction – the film *The Sting* starring Paul Newman and Robert Redford. In this story, a man is fooled into betting a huge amount of money on a horse that was a 'certainty' – the amount the man put on the horse (and lost) was called his stake.

Some people place everything they own (house, car, clothes, etc.) in a business that they believe will succeed. If it works, they have the satisfaction first of all of not losing anything and, secondly, making a profit. If you make big sacrifices (your stake) in order to create a successful business, you will expect to have a say in what happens from then on.

Types of stakeholder	
Owner	Ted Turner (CNN), Richard Branson (Virgin)
Shareholder	you, Duke of Westminster
Creditor	someone waiting to be paid
Debtor	someone who owes you money
Customer	buyers or users of your product
Government – tax	income tax, VAT, Customs and Excise
Government – law	Health and Safety, British Standards, discrimination
Manager	employed to take responsibility and make decisions
Employee	employed to carry out specific tasks
Supplier	provides the business with goods and services
Local community	the business is a part of the local environment
Trade unions	have the welfare of members as their business
Other groups	pressure groups – the 'antis', environmental organisations
European Union	special funding, grants, laws

To help understand the differing demands made on a business, we need to focus on four of the above.

The **customer** is the most important stakeholder and must be served with what he or she wants or there is no business. Remember the phrase, 'The customer is always right.' The best example is you – every time you shop or watch TV or go to the dentist, you are letting the world know what your needs and wants are. There should be someone there to meet your demands.

The **employee** can be hired and fired, but happy, motivated workers provide the best product in any business. It is well-known that a relaxed, supportive group of people can achieve a lot more than people who are being 'bullied' into working in a certain way. The big puzzle is how to achieve this at 'work', which most of us have to do to make a living.

The **shareholder** must see their share price increase they must receive a good return (dividend) on their investment (share) at the end of each year. A business that is making losses will find its shares dropping in price and in popularity. It will not be able to pay dividends (rewards for having shares) and it will be worth less on the stock market. Not many people will want to continue supporting this business.

A **pressure group** is a more complex stakeholder, since it is not directly involved. However, it has an increasingly effective voice in the market place and has already made a difference in major areas of the business world.

Examples are anti-capitalists disrupting normal life and making headlines, anti-abortion activists closing down clinics, anti-vivisectionists closing down laboratories and frightening off big banks, and environmentalists affecting how oil rigs are disposed of in the North Sea.

Test your knowledge and understanding

8.1 Achieve your goals

1. Name five basic objectives any business might have.
2. Name two advanced objectives.
3. Give one objective of a sole trader.
4. Give one objective of a partnership.
5. Give one objective of a private limited company.
6. Give one objective of a public limited company.
7. Give one objective of a charity.
8. Give one objective of a co-operative.
9. Give one objective of a franchise.
10. Give one objective of a voluntary organisation.

8.2 Measuring success

1. Explain the owner's interest in a business.
2. Explain a manager's interest in a business.
3. Explain the special position a sole trader is in.
4. Explain the employee's interest in a business.
5. Explain the shareholder's interest in a business.
6. Describe the difference in attitude between private and public company shareholders.
7. Name four types of stakeholder.
8. What do all stakeholders want?

8.3 Stakeholders

1. Describe how a private sector business measures its success.
2. Describe how a public sector business measures its success.
3. Describe how a voluntary business measures its success.
4. Explain what a stake in a business is.
5. Give five (very different) types of stakeholder and give an example of each. Do not use the examples in (6) below.
6. Expand your description of a customer, an employee and a pressure group.

1. As the recently appointed Chief Executive of Warp Speed Computers you have been asked to outline your goals. Prepare a presentation outlining your vision of the future for your press conference.

2. In what ways could the objectives of a sole trader and a plc be:
   a similar
   b different?
   Give reasons for your answers.

3. In what ways may the needs of employees differ from those of employers? How can you bring these groups together to ensure that the organisation meets its goals?

4.

   Rooms With a View plc announces record profits ...

   Sandy Shores Hotel wins award for customer service ...

   WE HELP delighted with levels of donations ...

   Each of these headlines announces good news. Find a range of headlines and match those to possible objectives of businesses or organisations. Use newspapers, the internet or magazines to find this information.

5. Prepare a spider diagram/mind map showing the range of possible stakeholders in each of the following types of organisations:
   a profit making
   b charity
   c local government.

Section 3

The resources businesses use

- Why do businesses locate where they do?
- How do people contribute to businesses?
- How do businesses use information?
- How do businesses operate?
- What challenges face businesses?

Why do businesses locate where they do?

In this unit you will learn about:

- where businesses locate
- why businesses locate where they do
- factors influencing location – market, resources, infrastructure
- where the money comes from – owners, borrowers
- sources of finance and government assistance
- globalisation.

9.1 / Deciding where to locate your business

Visit any city centre and you will find examples of entrepreneurs, usually in the right place at the right time. The reasons for their success could be: busy area, therefore customers are available; customer contact – a direct message is given to potential customers; low overhead costs leading to 'bargain prices'.

From this example we can find reasons explaining why businesses locate where they do. When a business is starting off, or expanding its sales horizons, a host of factors must be taken into consideration. These factors will vary in importance depending on the nature of the business in question.

Retailers need to be close to their market

Factors

- close to source of raw materials
- close to market
- skilled labour force available
- close to suppliers
- good infrastructure in place – rail, road, air links
- support available (funding/training)

Historical factors

A main historical factor for a business locating in a particular area was the availability of a source of raw materials, e.g. coal mines.

Another was being close to its market, i.e. where products and services could be sold directly to customers in the local area.

A further reason might be that people had particular skills in a particular area, therefore businesses would set up in that area to use the local expertise built up over a period of time.

Also, being close to your supplier used to be very important when setting up your business. This allowed easy access to the materials required and also kept transport costs down.

Modern factors

The more 'modern' reasons are similar. Globalisation and the development of **infrastructures** using air, road, rail and communication networks has led to business being much more mobile so that location is now regarded as a 'cost' decision, but the historical factors above still have a role to play.

Case study

Silicon Chip Co. is located in the central belt beside a large number of high-tech businesses. Consider the reasons for this:

● close to skilled labour – highly trained and skilled people providing a pool of labour to support new businesses

● close to suppliers – companies set up business in the area to provide supplies/support to other organisations

● close to market – goods will be transported throughout the world given that high-tech industries operate in a **global market**. An important point to note here is the quality of the infrastructure in attracting potential investors into the area. This relates to the quality of air, road, rail and communication links.

Where would you set up a fish farm?

A large number of salmon farms are located close to sources of materials – e.g. sea lochs around coastal areas. Skilled labour will be attracted into that area in search of employment. These farms are not near their markets. Products will be shipped worldwide using the latest packaging techniques, ensuring that quality produce is distributed using the most efficient transport methods linked to infrastructure. Farms are close to supplies, but not necessarily suppliers – by using modern infrastructure links, supplies can be obtained relatively easily.

One of the most vital things you need to do to get your business off the ground is to raise money in advance. How much you will need depends on the nature of your business. From your initial research, and from your business plan, you will have a fairly clear idea of what you need.

All new businesses require financial support. This support comes from a range of sources and will very much depend on the nature, type and size of business. The following extracts from the Scottish Enterprise website give information on finance available to support business.

Loan finance

This is the main form of external finance for new business, accounting for around 40% of the total. Nearly all of this comes from the banks, although loans on attractive rates may also be available from local authorities and specialist organisations like the Prince's Scottish Youth Business Trust (PSYBT) which specialises in loans to the under-25s. Getting loan finance depends on a number of things:

- your prospects for generating revenue over the medium term
- the security you are able to provide, and above all,
- the credibility of you and your business plan.

The main concern of a lender is your ability to repay the loan and meet the interest charges.

Equity capital

This is the financial foundation of your company. Equity is the core capital of the business: the money that helps to set up and sustain the business. A healthy base of equity finance can help unlock other sources, like bank loans or grants. It includes the money you put in yourself to the business, along with finance you can raise from informal sources like family and friends.

Grants

The third source of finance for a business is grants. One of the great myths of business in Scotland is that grants are freely available for people interested in trying to start a business. The reality is far from this. Only around 6% of the money that goes to new businesses comes from grants, and much of this will go to more substantial businesses with the prospects of employing significant numbers within a relatively short period. Grants are likely to be a top-up that meets any gaps on top of the other sources.

Your chances of securing support are dependent on a number of factors, including the long-term potential of the business and its likely contribution to the economy (e.g. in terms of jobs or the development of new industries).

Summary of possible sources of finance

Owners

The owner of a business can use his or her own personal money to invest in the business. This could come from savings, returns from investments, redundancy money or inheritance money.

Banks

By presenting your business plan you are providing banks with the opportunity to 'invest' in your business idea – either as start-up or as development. The banks will consider your business plan and assess the viability of the business and offer support (or not). Such a decision will consider the level of risk involved – is the business idea sound? Will the business prosper? Will the business be able to compete in the market place? These decisions will be based upon the previous experience of the banks as well as being influenced by the quality of the business plan. As well as financial support, banks will offer a range of business services, including financial advice, as part of a package.

Investors

If you present your business plan to potential investors they may decide to invest in your business. Since they will put money into your business, they will have a 'stake' in the business and will expect something back on their investment over a period of time. Investors are one of many stakeholders in your business.

Family and friends

This is a common source of 'business start-up' money. A family member recognises the potential of the idea and is keen to support the person to help them to get going – and looks forward to substantial profits in the future!

Government grants

The government also offers support at times to help stimulate economic activity in particular areas or sectors of business. This is available on a national and local scale – here are some examples from East Ayrshire Council:

DEPARTMENTS
DEVELOPMENT SERVICES
ECONOMIC DEVELOPMENT

West of Scotland Loan Fund

This is a loan scheme to provide finance to new and existing businesses in East Ayrshire. The Council will not be sole funder of a project but will operate in conjunction with other lending agencies.

The West of Scotland Loan Fund aims to encourage the creation and growth of small businesses which can contribute to the East Ayrshire economy in terms of jobs, growth potential etc. The scheme is primarily targeted at small companies involved in manufacturing, however, service sector companies can also apply. Retail businesses are not normally supported through this scheme.

DEPARTMENTS
DEVELOPMENT SERVICES
ECONOMIC DEVELOPMENT

Grants and Loans - We're Here to Help

The staff of Economic Development section of East Ayrshire Council will help you make sense of the funding available to you through grants and loans. These pages will give you an idea of the assistance you may be entitled to, however, why not contact us to discuss the individual needs of your business.

Venture capital companies

This type of business is always on the look-out to invest in potentially profitable businesses in need of development funding. Successful new businesses can lead to good returns for venture capital companies.

Other sources of finance

Further forms of financial support can be found from other sources.

Business start-up schemes

Local authorities offer a variety of advice services, such as running courses to support new business ideas and helping people to develop their ideas into a working business opportunity. These courses may also provide basic training in aspects of finance, marketing, human resources and business planning.

Enterprise companies

These organisations will support the start-up schemes above, providing a resource for new businesses to tap into and offering practical working advice based upon previous experience. Scottish Enterprise is one such organisation offering on-line support to new businesses.

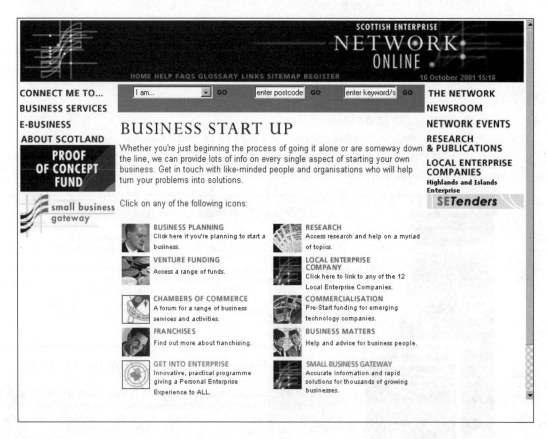

Chambers of Commerce

These offer a discussion forum for business services and activities at a local level, e.g. Ayrshire Chamber of Commerce.

Small Business Gateway

Organisations such as this offer a range of support services and advice for new and developing businesses.

European Union funding

The European Union is a possible resource for businesses attempting to gain necessary funding for the development of new ideas. A number of different funds can be accessed to assist the business and its development.

The Prince's Trust

This is a charity providing funding to support new business ideas and opportunities and is aimed at the under-25s.

Internet

The **internet** provides a wealth of information – any business advice you require is out there just waiting to be accessed!

Did you know?

- During 2000 a total of 17,114 new businesses were created in Scotland.
- During the same period 11,623 business closures were recorded!

From this information, it is clear that support is readily available and always required – even with this support sometimes businesses can fail!

9.3 The global market

Gone are the days when firms operated within restricted boundaries – today a very large number of firms operate within a **global market**. The progress made as a result of ICT developments has led to markets becoming global for more companies than ever before. Some examples of global companies are Coca-Cola, Ford and Heinz. The products of these organisations are produced and sold throughout the world. The ever-increasing pace of e-commerce has further developed the concept of globalisation. Using the internet, companies can set up global shops, whereby their products can be distributed throughout the world.

Advantages of being a global company

- larger market – wider range of customers
- more resources available – money, employees, equipment
- economies of scale (see Unit 5).

Disadvantages of being a global company

- communication issues – language, distance (overcome by ICT?)
- diseconomies of scale (see Unit 5)
- market fluctuations – different markets will experience different conditions
- cultural differences – complexity of international business is highlighted by different approaches to work/society in different countries.

Case study

Supermarkets 'must go global'

Food retailers will need to go global to succeed, Tesco, the UK's largest supermarket chain, has said in announcing half-year profits up 10.2%.

Consolidation among supermarkets in leading nations and sales growth in emerging markets will prompt leading store chains to take an international outlook, said Tesco, which plans to run 130 hypermarkets abroad by 2002.

Tesco, announcing group sales up 10.7% to £10.1bn between March and August, also claimed to be the world's largest internet grocery business, with 750,000 registered customers and orders running at £60,000 per week.

Terry Leahy, Tesco's chief executive, said: 'These are strong results, reflecting the successful implementation of our strategy. Tesco is moving from being a domestic player to being an international retailer of real scale, giving us a strong position in the league of major international retailers.'

International giant

Successful retailers will be those which can manage changes in domestic and foreign markets to emerge as global forces, says the company statement, which predicts that 45% of Tesco's shopping space will be outside the UK by 2002.

The statement also confirmed earlier reports that the group will create 20,000 jobs worldwide this year.

Tesco's overall international sales rose 42% to £1.2bn over the six months, with revenue from Asian and central European operations almost doubling.

Overseas stores (to end 2000)

Czech Rep and Slovakia: 11	Hungary: 15
Poland: 10	South Korea: 3
Taiwan: 1	Thailand: 24

By the end of 2000, the food giant will operate 15 hypermarkets in Hungary, Tesco's key central European market, with 10 outlets open in Poland.

The company plans to run 61 hypermarkets in Asia by the end of 2002, with 32 open now in South Korea, Thailand, one planned for Taiwan, and company officials investigating opportunities in Malaysia, Japan and China.

In the UK, where Tesco is opening 30 stores this year, sales rose 7.5% to £8.9bn despite 'intense competition for customers'.

All but three of the new stores will be built on brownfield sites, the company said.

Tesco shares stood 14.5p up at 221p in afternoon trade in London.

Source: BBC News Online (19 September 2000)

Questions

1. What are the benefits of supermarkets 'going global'?
2. What drawbacks may be encountered by supermarkets considering global issues?
3. What impact have internet sales had on Tesco?
4. What factors will Tesco consider when locating stores?
5. How will Tesco fund its expansion plans?
6. Suggest reasons why Tesco's share price has increased.

Test your knowledge and understanding

9.1 Deciding where to locate your business

1. Give five reasons why businesses may locate in a particular area.
2. Explain what is meant by the term 'infrastructure'.
3. Give three reasons why Silicon Chip Co. decided to set up in this location.
4. Why does the availability of a trained workforce attract business to a particular location?

9.2 Sources of financial support

1. Describe the possible sources of funds for a new business venture.
2. Why do people invest money in businesses?
3. What is the meaning of the term 'stakeholder'?
4. Name and describe three sources of support for a developing business.

9.3 The global market

1. Name five global companies.
2. Explain the meaning of the term 'globalisation'.
3. What are the benefits of being a global company?
4. What are the drawbacks of being a global business?

Test your decision-making skills

1. You want to start up in business selling designer clothes. What factors might you consider when deciding on a location for your outlet?
2. Using a local example, prepare a brief presentation clearly stating the reasons for this location decision. Choose from the following options:
   a presentation to class
   b prepare a handout for your class
   c use presentation software, e.g. PowerPoint.
3. As a business support agency, what advice would you offer to a client who is preparing to meet with a potential investor (who incidentally has pots of money!)?
4. Access the internet to find out details about your local enterprise company. From the information you find, prepare a report to include details about the range of activities it is involved in – particularly those relating to supporting new businesses.
5. As a Consultant with NewBiz Developments, you have been contracted to offer advice to your client on business planning. Prepare a skeleton business plan that you can complete with your client. (Remember – quality counts!)

6 In your position as Managing Director, you are required to prepare a case in favour of developing the business worldwide. Present your case to the class, ensuring that they get the message.

UNIT 10 / How do people contribute to businesses?

In this unit you will learn about:

- why people work
- choosing the right person for the job
- job/person specifications
- selection and recruitment (internal and external)
- full-time, part-time, permanent and temporary staff
- manual and skilled staff
- the role of appraisal
- relationships between employees and employers
- changing patterns of employment.

10.1 / Why do people work?

People work for many reasons – for security, for money, even for fun! The basic reason is to provide for themselves or their families – you may recognise this since this is satisfying basic needs and wants, i.e. the provision of food, clothing, etc. People are central to the success of any business – the better the people, the better the chances of the business being successful.

If this is the case, how do firms find the 'right people'?

- Is there such a thing as the right person?
- Does the perfect employee exist?
- Can employees be improved?
- Do conditions affect employees?

The human resources function of the business will generally be responsible for this task of finding the right people. They will work in close liaison with the departments for whom new employees are needed.

10.2 / Choosing the right person for the job

Selection process

❶ vacancy arises – need for employee is recognised
❷ job specification prepared
❸ job description prepared
❹ person specification prepared
❺ vacancy advertised – internally/externally

❻ applications received
❼ interviews arranged – variety of methods used
❽ choice of new employee made
❾ induction training for new employee

Firms will try to find the right person for any particular vacancy or need within their structure. To do this they need to design a **job specification** containing the key elements of the work to be done. From this a **job description** is created which would be made available to potential employees, acting as a summary of the job. A **person specification** is also prepared showing a) the **essential** and b) the **desirable** qualities of the type of person the company is looking for.

Job Description

Company:
Future Vision

Job title:
Marketing Executive

Purpose of job:
To assist in customer relationships, brand loyalty incentives, web presence, reports and presentations.

Specific duties:
a)   Maintain customer relations management database.
b)   Prepare and present reports at weekly marketing meetings.
c)   Take overall responsibility for marketing information on company website.

Other responsibilities:
Supervise the Marketing Assistant.

Location:
Inverness

Responsible to:
Marketing Manager

Application forms

Businesses may have application forms they can issue to potential employees. Applicants for the job complete the form, which asks for basic personal information as well as more searching questions, allowing the business to build up a picture of the applicant. An increasing number of companies now have application forms available on their website which can be downloaded, completed by the applicant and returned via e-mail.

Future Vision

APPLICATION FOR THE POST OF Marketing Executive	REFERENCE No FV001

FAMILY NAME Robertson	FIRST NAMES (in full) Fraser

POSTAL ADDRESS (including postcode) 81 Town Road Parkside Glasgow G2 8UL	TITLE (Dr, Mr, Ms etc) Mr	DATE OF BIRTH 24/07/1975
	NATIONALITY British	MALE/FEMALE Male
	HOME TELEPHONE/ MOBILE 0141 123 456	WORK TELEPHONE/FAX 0141 567 891
	EMAIL ADDRESS fraser@ezemail.co.uk	

EDUCATION *(Secondary, Further and Higher Education)*

From	To	School/College/University	Qualification/Subject
1985	1991	Kennedy School	7 Standard Grades 2 Higher Grades
1991	1993	Parkview College	HND Marketing (merit)

EMPLOYMENT HISTORY *(Chronological Order)*

From	To	Employer	Post Held
1994	1996	NRG Solutions	Customer Services Assistant
1996	1999	Focus Interactive	Marketing Administrator
1999	present	Focus Interactive	Marketing Officer

WORK AND OTHER RELEVANT EXPERIENCE

Describe briefly your work or other relevant experience, including any other statement in support of your application

I have been working in a marketing environment for five years, and am experienced in CRM and presenting reports at weekly marketing meetings.

I am currently taaking an evening course in Marketing on the Web and intend to focus on brand loyalty incentives as part of my coursework. I enjoy working as part of a team and have excellent communication and interpersonnal skills.

REFEREES

(name, address, telephone number)

1 Mr W Smith Personnel Manager NRG Solutions Glasgow G1 2BC	2 Mrs M Tsang Tutor, HND Marketing Parkview College College Road Glasgow G10 3AD

Curriculum vitae (CV)

In addition to the application form, some applicants may include their CV. This allows applicants to add more detail about their 'history', providing a further opportunity for the paper 'picture' of the applicant to be formed. Indeed some firms are now using ICT and developing video CVs thereby gaining an immediate impression of the person applying for the job!

Curriculum Vitae

Rasheda Zaher

Personal Details

Address: 4 Railway Street
          Aberdeen
          AB1 2CD

Telephone: (01224) 123456

Email: rasheda@abc.def.uk

Date of birth: 6 January 1973

Marital status: Single

Education and qualifications

Institution	Dates	Awards	Grade
Hillside School	1984 - 1990	8 Standard Grades:	
		English	1
		Maths	1
		Business Management	1
		French	2
		Geography	2
		Physics	3
		Biology	2
		Art	3
		4 Higher Grades:	
		Mathematics	A
		French	C
		Business Management	B
		English	B
FE College	1990 - 1991	SVQ Level II: Business Management	

Work experience

Employer	Dates	Job title
ABC Communications	1999 - present	IT Support Officer
Tech Directions Ltd	1994 - 1999	Helpdesk Assistant
XYZ Recruit	1991 - 1994	Office Junior

Interests

I am a keen golfer and also enjoy playing chess. I enjoy singing and am a member of a local pop group.

Interviews

An interview is where the business invites a selection of the applicants for the job to meet with representatives of the company. During the interview the candidate will be asked a series of questions which relate to the job and the applicant's experience.

Interviews vary in the way in which they are carried out, for example:

- **One-to-one** – this form of interview will only involve the interviewer and the interviewee.
- **Panel** – this will involve the candidate and a selection panel. Panels are made up of staff involved in different areas of the business.
- **Group interviews** – in this format the candidates are asked to work as a group and are assessed in terms of their performance within the group.
- **First round/second round interviews** – a first round of interviews may be used to eliminate some candidates; those remaining are invited back for further interview. During the second round more searching questions/activities are used to find out as much as possible about the candidate's knowledge, skills and personality.

Internal or external appointments?

Some businesses carry out the selection process from within the business, i.e. the human resources function organises it throughout the business. An alternative to this is to use an outside recruitment agency to find the right people for you.

Some businesses will promote staff from within the organisation, recognising skills, loyalty, ambition and flair. Others will bring people in from other businesses, with the view that new ideas and ways of working can be brought into the business from outside.

Training

An athlete trains for four years in search of Olympic glory – this requires continual practice and the development of the appropriate skills and techniques. When that 'Olympic moment' comes along the athlete is at peak fitness.

In a business sense, employees should be producing the best possible quality of goods or services. To do this requires training, i.e. the opportunity to practise and develop skills.

Training helps to keep employees motivated

Benefits of training

- keeps skills up to date
- allows the business to remain competitive
- helps motivate employees
- good for future employment prospects – helps attract new employees

Types of training

- **On-the-job training** – training while continuing to work; observation of fellow employees as they carry out their duties (**shadowing**).
- **Off-the-job training** – going on training courses held away from the workplace: conferences, college courses, etc.
- **Long-term training** – blocks of training taken over a longer time frame.

- **Impact training** – short, sharp sessions, e.g. preparation for a sales promotion campaign.
- **Strategic training** – this form of training would involve and affect the entire workforce.
- **Operational training** – this form of training would tackle specific aspects of the business.

By investing time and money into the development of employees, businesses can have greater confidence that their workforce/team is able to deliver to expected standards. An example would be **quality assurance** – all workers are trained to produce goods/services to the same quality standard.

10.3 Types of employees

The workforce of any business may be made up from a variety of 'types' of employees who will be working under different contracts and terms and conditions. The following are examples of the different kinds of employees:

- **Full time** – working full allocation of time as per contract, e.g. 35 hours per week.
- **Part time** – working only part of the agreed time allocation, e.g. 15 hours per week.
- **Permanent** – a permanent employee of the business; works within the boundaries of the employment contract and intends to have a long-term association with the organisation.
- **Temporary** – short-term contracts for employees who are only needed for shorter periods of time.
- **Skilled** – employees who have been trained in a particular area and have some form of professional training, e.g. electrician, nurse, plumber.
- **Manual** – employees who have not been trained in any particular area, but nonetheless contribute to the goals of the organisation, e.g. labourers on a building site.

Examples at your local supermarket will include:

- full-time permanent skilled staff, e.g. café supervisor
- part-time temporary staff, e.g. students working on a short-term basis for only part of the week.

10.4 Appraisal

How do you know your employees are doing their job well? How do your employees know they are doing their job well?

These questions lead us on to the concept of appraisal. Appraisal is often regarded as an emotional term. It involves a 'two-way' discussion between employees who operate at different levels in an organisation. Meetings to assess employee performance and progress will be held on a regular basis – this will differ from business to business, e.g. once a year, twice a year, etc.

These meetings can have an impact on the work of the employee in many ways, for example:

- Employees might receive revised pay and conditions within the firm's bandings/limits.
- Employees could be set quality or production targets.
- Employees could raise any worries or issues that they have.
- Employers could identify areas for improvement that they would expect to see from the employee.
- Employers could take the opportunity to praise employees for good work.

Benefits

By actively involving the employee in this discussion, the business and the employee have the opportunity to openly and regularly discuss issues, helping to ensure that good communication between employees and employers helps the business to meet its goals.

Drawbacks

Sometimes employees feel threatened by the appraisal process. They may feel that the person who appraises them is unfair, does not like them, or 'has it in for them'. They may also see the process as a chance for the business to reduce the workforce or give employees more work to complete (more responsibility, but no increase in financial reward!). Employees may lack confidence to express themselves and therefore miss out on the opportunity to say what they really think, or to give themselves enough credit for what they do.

Reflection

As mentioned above, the business is only as good as the people it employs. Employees who are given the opportunity to have their views heard and have positive and constructive comments from their employers are likely to be more highly motivated, leading to a greater chance of success for all concerned.

Let's briefly consider two examples.

- If employees are not valued and do not have their views taken into account, they are less likely to be motivated to work hard and do well for themselves or the business.
- If the relationship between employers and employees is good then there is a greater chance for the company to meet a range of challenges.

> **Did you know?**
>
> On average, workers are likely to experience up to five job changes during their working lives!

Change, change and yet more change!

The changing nature of work is driven by the changing needs of the business. As more and more capital is invested in technology, traditional working roles are constantly being modified. Technology used in the right way can be an extremely valuable tool in the workplace – a key benefit is the release of time for the individual either to do different work, or to have more leisure time. Some examples of how technology has changed the way we work can be highlighted by the following examples.

Growth in home working

Why travel to the office when you can be connected at home using telephones and computers? You can access your office files from the comfort of your own home – no traffic, no cold and wet mornings, etc. It sounds great: the only thing missing is people! You may be distracted less, but may miss the opportunity to discuss ideas with your colleagues face to face.

Hot-desking

In this form of working environment you do not have your 'own' space – you use areas as required. The key issue is flexibility of the workplace and the workforce. Find a space and use it – then move on to your next task. A focus of this form of working is getting the job done – efficiently.

Working hours

The traditional office hours of 9 a.m. to 5 p.m. is a model that has changed and will continue to change to ensure that the combined needs of employees and employer can be met. Traditional systems have been replaced by **flexible working hours**. A set amount of time is built up over a given period of time, e.g. a week, or a month. A typical example of flexible working is:

Start	**Lunch**	**Finish**
08.00–10.00	12.00–14.00	16.00–18.00

You can start at any time within the set limits, have lunch anytime within the set limits, and finish likewise! Companies offer this flexible practice to counter travel congestion, help with child care and to see the benefits of more relaxed but motivated employees.

Short-term and fixed-term contracts

More and more organisations are employing people on the basis of need. Six-month or twelve-month contracts with specific objectives ensure that work that needs to be done is done! The benefit to the employer is that the person is not a permanent member of staff and overall costs (pension contributions, company cars, etc.) can be reduced, although you may pay this form of employee at higher rates.

A further benefit of employing **contractors** on a short-term basis is the chance to bring in specialists to tackle problems, offering a range of solutions based upon their experiences elsewhere. (See Unit 16 for more on problem-solving and decision-making.)

Test your knowledge and understanding

10.1 Why do people work?

❶ Describe the role of the functional area of business responsible for finding the right employee.

❷ Suggest three reasons to explain why people work.

10.2 Choosing the right person for the job

❶ Does quality guarantee success?

❷ Describe three different forms of interview.

❸ Why might a firm decide to appoint someone from outside the organisation?

❹ What are the main benefits of training?

❺ Describe four forms of training.

10.3 Types of employees

❶ Name five different types of worker.

10.4 Appraisal

❶ Explain the meaning of the term 'appraisal'.

❷ Describe the possible impact of appraisal on both employees and the organisations they work for.

10.5 The effect of new technology on business

❶ How has technology changed the way we work?

❷ Explain the meaning of the following:
   a home working
   b flexible working hours
   c hot-desking

❸ What are the benefits of employing staff on fixed-term contracts?

Test your decision-making skills

❶ As Human Resources Manager you have been asked to redesign the job application form used by the company. What information will you ask for? Prepare a draft copy for discussion in your group.

❷ Prepare your curriculum vitae (CV).

❸ As part of an interview panel set up to appoint a new Training and Development Manager, you are required to prepare five questions in advance of the interview. What questions will you ask?

❹ As a Training Officer, how would you develop the ICT skills of employees?

❺ Some employees feel threatened by appraisal – how would you overcome this?

❻ With a focus on recruitment, search the internet for examples of information from multi-national businesses. Present your findings to the rest of the class.

In this unit you will learn about:

- what information is and where it comes from
- internal and external sources
- using computers to generate information – spreadsheets, databases, desktop publishing, word processing and networks
- the flow of information
- using information to monitor and control the business.

11.1 / What is information?

Information is presented in a variety of ways. In a business the same principle applies. Information is generated from within the business and also from external sources, e.g. customers, suppliers, surveys, competitors, etc. Businesses must use the information to make decisions that affect its future prosperity, which will have an impact on employees, shareholders, customers and, indeed, competitors.

Information is often described as the life-blood of any organisation – let's find out if this is true! Information can be split into two types – internal and external.

Internal information is generated from within the business. Examples of internal information are company reports on various aspects of business activity, e.g. sales reports, financial information, internal e-mails, minutes from department meetings, company newsletters and employees' views.

External information is generated from outside the business, but affects the business in a variety of ways depending on the kind of information. Examples of external information are consumer surveys, press articles, information from suppliers and customer feedback forms/complaints. The internet is a useful business tool to keep track of competitors to ensure that you are keeping up to date with them and challenging them in the best possible way.

By considering the range of information generated from all of these internal and external sources, it is clear to see how important information is to any business. But how good and how useful is the information you use? This is extremely important in determining the success of the business!

If information is to be used to assist the business the following qualities should be considered. Good quality information should be as follows:

- **Relevant** – information should relate to the intended purpose.
- **Accurate** – information should not be misleading or contain errors, e.g. financial figures should be correct.
- **Cost effective** – information is a resource used by business, but it should be remembered that it costs money to generate information in a suitable format. The intended use of the information should be taken into account as should the cost of getting it, e.g. costs of customer surveys, time and staff costs involved in finding out customer opinion, etc.
- **Timely** – when information is available or presented is clearly important. Information should be available before decisions are taken. If it is not available on time then its value is very limited, but the right information at the right time is a very useful business resource.
- **Concise** – why have a fifty-page report when a fifteen-page report could cover the same points? The people who have to read and use the information require quality information, not information hidden in a wordy report.
- **Meaningful** – the people who read the information should have no difficulty in understanding it. The information should be clear and easily understood by the intended users.
- **Up to date** – the information used to make decisions should be 'fresh' and not past its sell by date. The business could suffer if decisions are based on old, out-of-date information, e.g. investment decisions based on old data.

Decisions taken by a business are based on information – the better the quality of the information available, the better the chance of the right decision. Decisions will be based on internal information, external information and a combination of internal and external sources.

The benefits of new technology

A major source of information is the huge volume generated by computers. Software packages used on computers perform a range of functions to help businesses meet their diverse aims and goals.

Benefits of computer-generated information

Computer-generated information is produced more quickly than by more traditional methods, and can then be amended to suit particular needs. A greater volume of information also becomes available to assist the organisation via the internet.

More people have easier access to both internal and external information – the use of e-mail, intranets and networks within organisations makes the information available and accessible both to employees and to stakeholders in the business.

Spreadsheets

	A	B	C	D
1	Area	Sales Units	Unit Price	Revenue
2	Aberdeen	200254	0.89	£178,226.06
3	Edinburgh	352178	0.89	£313,438.42
4	Glasgow	399658	0.89	£355,695.62
5	Stirling	145057	0.89	£129,100.73
6	Dumfries	125001	0.89	£111,250.89

A spreadsheet is an electronic grid where information is entered, organised and manipulated. Common uses for spreadsheets lie in the financial areas of a business: the preparation of accounting information, salary and wage calculations, etc. Number information can be presented in chart and graph form making it easier to understand and therefore perhaps more useful in assisting in the decision-making process of the business.

Databases

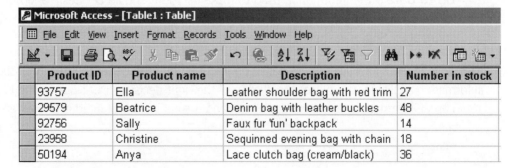

Databases are electronic forms of storing information. Records are created and can be stored, edited and updated easily leading to greater efficiency for the business. Examples of databases in a business are employee records, stock records, and sales records.

Desktop publishing

Desktop publishing software allows information to be presented in attractive, eye-catching ways, which gives the information an image suitable for its intended purpose. Desktop publishing software can be used to prepare reports, business plans, brochures, flyers and notices, and these can be used both internally and externally.

Smart Cookies Company News

This month
- Employee of the month
- Glasgow sales boom
- Training courses – dates and details

Word processing

Word-processing software allows information to be entered into the computer, stored on disk, edited, formatted and printed. This allows information to be made available in a readable, quality format for both internal and external uses. Common uses of word-processing software include preparation of letters and business reports.

E-mail

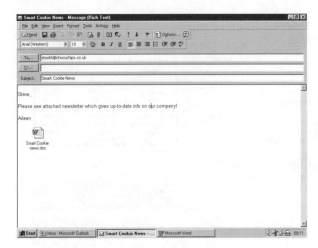

Did you know?

Did you know that e-mail travels at 3,000 miles per second . . . and it's getting faster!

The speed of exchanging messages and information between computers on a worldwide scale makes e-mail an extremely useful software application for any business. Messages can be sent between individuals, groups of people in a business or between businesses which leads to more effective communication all round (if the system is used and managed properly!). As well as basic messages, files, pictures and reports can be attached to e-mails making them even more powerful for business activity and communication.

Internet

The internet is a series of connected networks which share and exchange information, routing requests for information to computers around the world. A large percentage of businesses have their own website which they use to promote the business by providing information about products, services, special offers, etc. Large numbers of businesses also sell directly from their website, offering the company a further retail outlet in addition to existing methods of selling, such as shops and mail order.

Networks

Networks link various parts of a business together through computers. Networks can be split into local area networks (within a building) or wide area networks that link different parts of an organisation together via a combination of joined computer networks. For example, Thomas Cook branches are all joined together electronically.

Case study

Thomas Cook is a well-known high street travel agent which deals with all aspects of the holiday business from sales and advice, to bookings and foreign exchange.

Thomas Cook as a business will use information on a daily basis from both internal and external sources.

Key issues

● Quality of information – is it relevant, accurate, up to date, etc?

● Information is central to the decisions made by the company.

● Databases include customer details.

● Word processing includes letters to customers.

● Desktop publishing is used for adverts, posters, leaflets.

● As you can see above, you can find all kinds of information on the website as well as booking your holiday.

● Different areas of the business will use information in different ways.

● Technology will continually be updated to ensure an efficient service (as well as to keep up with the competition).

The flow of information

We make decision upon decision, day after day – all based on this wonderful commodity called information. We have established what information is, where it comes from, the role of information and communications technology in providing information, and what makes good information – but how does it all make sense?

Let's consider the following diagram:

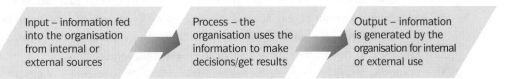

Input – information fed into the organisation from internal or external sources

Process – the organisation uses the information to make decisions/get results

Output – information is generated by the organisation for internal or external use

Depending on the nature of the decision, the level of the business it is made at and the expected impact of the decision, information goes into the organisation and is processed by a variety of people working in departments (Human Resources, Finance, Marketing, Operations). These people will work at different levels of responsibility and authority. The organisation will respond in various ways by, for example:

● keeping information within the business for future use
● passing information on from the business to customers, suppliers, etc.

Information 'flows' around the business and can indeed be regarded as the 'life-blood of the organisation' – without information the business cannot survive!

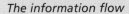

Case study

Heading in the right direction!

AZK is a leading car manufacturer. A rival car manufacturer launches a new car featuring satellite navigation as standard on all models in the range.

The information flow
The Marketing Director receives an e-mail from the Market Research team confirming competitor's move with new car and satellite navigation. She decides that the business must follow suit and also devise a counter-campaign to maintain sales of existing models.

The Operations Director needs to know this information to ensure that production can be suitably adjusted within a relatively quick timescale.

The Finance Department needs to make decisions related to costs of production, marketing costs, selling prices for revised cars, etc.

The Human Resources staff will need to ensure that workers have the skills and training necessary to cope with the production line change.

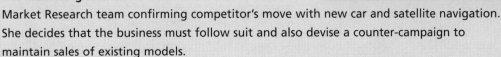

The business response will have to take account of the views of this range of staff – just imagine how the information would flow around the business taking the form of e-mails, reports, financial statements, sales graphs, production schedules, etc.

- If the business is to survive and prosper it must take in information, make sense of it and respond by making the 'right decision', whatever that may be!
- How do you know if you made the right decision? Surprise, surprise – you need yet more information!
- Whatever decision you take, you must evaluate the effects of your decision. The flow of information continues, e.g. sales levels and customer responses, which can be analysed by each functional area of the business using ICT to break down the information and present it in the most suitable format for those who require it.
- In summary, the relationship between information, decision-making and ICT are central to the success of any business.

Test your knowledge and understanding

11.1 What is information?

1. What is information?
2. Why is information presented in different ways?
3. Distinguish between internal and external information.
4. Describe five features of 'good' information.

11.2 The benefits of new technology

1. What are the benefits of computer-generated information?
2. Describe the features and uses of five main software applications.
3. What are the benefits of a network?

11.3 The flow of information

1. Give an example of the input, process and output stages of a decision made by a business.
2. Describe the role of ICT in information processing.
3. From the case study 'Heading in the right direction' what information was required by each of the four functional areas?
4. Why is it important to evaluate decisions?
5. Why is information often referred to as a 'flow'?

Test your decision-making skills

1. Use a graphics/desktop publishing package to prepare a diagram showing the qualities of 'good information'.
2. Prepare a presentation to convince your colleagues of the benefits of computer-generated information. Choose from the following options:
   - standard presentation
   - handout
   - electronic presentation (PowerPoint).
3. Compare the websites of two well-known businesses such as the Virgin Group and Debenhams plc. Prepare a bullet list of your findings.
4. Your business is reviewing its advertising campaign. On what kinds of information will decisions be based? Use an input, process, output model to explain your answer.
5. What are the key areas that influence the quality of information available to businesses?

UNIT 12 / How do businesses operate?

In this unit you will learn about:

- how businesses make products (input, process, output)
- job production
- batch production
- flow production
- people versus machines
- quality assurance
- stock control
- methods of distribution.

12.1 / The production process

In everyday life we take so much for granted – for instance, the humble, ordinary, household carpets that we walk on! Wool carpets start off as something quite different: a carpet starts its **production cycle** as a sheep!

The following is an example of a production process by a yarn producing company who supply a range of quality carpet manufacturers.

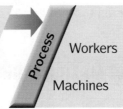

Input	Process	Output
Raw materials Man-made Natural	Workers Machines	Quality yarn to produce carpets

Production process

Input   A combination of natural and man-made fibres are mixed together at the start of the process. This is the first stage in the production of yarn.

Process   The combined raw materials (inputs) are then worked on by a combination of machines and workers who operate the machines. During this stage in the production process the inputs are changed to become ready for sale, i.e. inputs are processed to become outputs.

Output   At this final stage in the production process the product is ready for distribution to customers. In this case cones of high quality yarn will be shipped worldwide to carpet manufacturers allowing the production of miles of carpets.

From this example it is clear that the business must have an effective system of producing goods – this is the functional area called **operations**.

Production mix

The production mix, which combines inputs, processes and outputs – IPO – is the way in which goods are produced ready for delivery to customers.

All products can be examined to establish inputs, processes and outputs – from plant seeds to flowers; plastic, chips, glass, etc. to a PC!

Obviously the nature and balance of inputs, processes and outputs will differ greatly given the diversity of products and services available globally today. However, even within the same industry, the balance of inputs, processes and outputs will vary depending on design, quality and costs associated with the product and the company – a car is a car but a small family car is different from a luxury 4x4!

12.2 Job, batch and flow production

There are three main methods used in the production of goods – job production, batch production and flow production techniques.

Job production

Job production techniques are used when the item is specifically designed or built to order, e.g. a custom-fitted bedroom, oil rigs, individually designed clothes, or a luxury yacht.

Advantages
- high quality – skilled workers produce quality work
- workers more highly motivated – sense of pride

Disadvantages
- labour intensive – leading to higher wage costs
- less chance of automation
- expensive production technique

Batch production

Batch production techniques are used when groups of products are made at the same time. An example is a baker making trays of bread rolls – first the mix of dough is made, then shapes cut out and placed on baking trays and finally cooked in the oven as a batch.

Advantages
- workers can specialise in one particular area
- lower costs per production unit

Disadvantages
- holding stock costs money
- time delays – resetting/cleaning equipment before next batch can start
- reduced motivation – employees are doing same job all the time

Flow production

Flow production techniques are used when large volumes of goods are being produced. A common example would be car production, when production line techniques are used – a basic frame goes on at the start of the line, finishing with the completed car ready to roll off the end of the line.

Advantages
- large numbers of products made at one time
- a chance to use machines, which will bring down wage costs

Disadvantages
- set-up costs are high – lots of equipment required
- employee motivation lower – monotonous jobs day-in, day-out
- interdependence – if one part of the production line goes wrong, the rest of the line is also affected

12.3 Human versus machine

When producing goods, businesses strive for efficiency. Major factors considered are those of quality and cost. As soon as you mention these variables it is important to consider the human versus machine debate.

> 'One machine can do the work of 50 ordinary men. No machine can do the work of one extraordinary man!'
>
> Elbert Hubbard (1856–1915), American businessman, writer and printer.

We can look at both humans and machines to compare their strengths and weaknesses.

Human		Machine	

+	-	+	-
skill	wage costs	tirelessness	maintenance
brainpower	interdependence	accuracy	interdependence
problem solving	time limits	consistency	lack of flexibility
interaction	physical limits		
adaptability			

When looking at job production techniques we established that the individualised nature of the products would often rely on highly skilled manual input. Businesses often look for the combination of human and machine, thereby gaining the best of both worlds. If a machine can produce goods efficiently and effectively, then human labour can be employed to support the machine.

12.4 Quality control

Tick in the box

> 'Quality is remembered long after the price is forgotten.'
>
> Gucci family slogan

This statement is obvious, but quality is the key to success for any business.

If you receive poor service you might tell ten people about your negative experience – if you receive good service you might only tell one person! Therefore to ensure your business maintains a good reputation it is clear that 'getting it right' is a key issue.

Quality models

A number of quality models are used within businesses – again, the nature and type of the business will determine the model adopted by the business.

Some examples include:

- total quality management
- quality improvement teams
- quality circles
- customer feedback schemes

Total quality management

In this quality model, everyone in the chain (i.e. each and every person involved in the production of a good) is regarded as your customer. The person who buys the good or uses the service is a 'customer'. With total quality management, everyone is aware of their responsibility in terms of quality. Clear definitions of quality are set out at each stage and all staff involved are aware of the objectives in relation to quality. Before they pass on a product to the next stage, they will be satisfied that they have got it right.

When organisations adopt a quality model, they use this information when promoting their goods or services. In a competitive market it is always a plus if you can highlight quality! For example, Scottish Beef's promotional campaign, Sony's worldwide reputation, etc.

Quality circles

A quality circle is a working group made up from a combination of management staff and employees with the objective of improving whatever they do. This joint group with a common goal will continually try to improve how things are done – this may result in lower costs as well as improved quality, and therefore higher profit levels.

Customer feedback schemes

One way of finding out what the all-important customers feel about a good or service is to continually ask for feedback. By finding out what the customer thinks, amendments can be made if necessary, ensuring that you are always in touch with the opinions of your customers. The internet is now a key method of gaining customer information – 'send in your details and opinions of our service!'

Stock control

No matter what method of production is used there must be a system of stock control, otherwise production would be extremely inefficient, unreliable and costly which is not good for business. Imagine the time wasted if certain key items were unavailable and production could not take place – for example, machines not being used, workers being paid to do 'nothing'. Stock control and stock management are key issues when determining the success of businesses.

Electronic point of sale (EPOS) stock control

Modern technology allows businesses not only to monitor stock, but to re-order stock and to gain marketing information about their customers, allowing efficiencies in stock management, financial management and marketing management. Computer systems monitor stock levels as items pass through the pay desk; these systems can automatically re-order when necessary as well as producing both sales and financial information. This all leads to better-informed decisions being taken.

Just-in-time

This is a system of stock management that ensures that the business has just enough stock to keep production going, so that no money is tied up in excess stock, leaving money available for other areas of the business. Modern production techniques mean that goods are made upon receipt of orders and not produced for stock – again this improves efficiency within the business and has an impact on the stock control systems used within the business.

Does ICT help?

ICT plays a central role in stock control. Databases are widely used to monitor stock levels, replacing more traditional manual methods. Stock systems can be updated on a regular basis and amendments made at the touch of a button. The information available can be searched and reports produced to assist in decision-making.

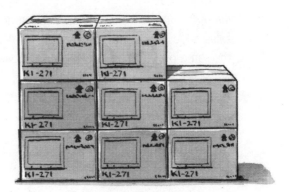

Distribution

The production of your goods or delivery of your service is clearly an essential ingredient in meeting goals and building success for the business. However, no matter how good your product or service is you must be equally efficient when it comes to the distribution of your product or delivery of your service. The actual method of delivery will vary depending on the physical nature of the products: their size, volume, value, the distances involved and the quantities.

Some distribution options

- Deliver direct to the customer.
- Supply to a wholesaler who can supply retailers.
- Supply to retailers who in turn supply to customers.
- Mail order systems of delivery.
- Online shopping via the internet.

Deliver direct to the customer – goods are produced and sent directly to customers who buy your products, e.g. custom-made furniture.

Supply to a wholesaler who supplies retailers – wholesaler, e.g. a fruit merchant, would buy a number of products with the intention of selling on to retailers/shops.

Supply to retailers who in turn supply to customers – your products are bought by retailers who sell them on to their customers, at a profit of course! Stores like the Co-op sell a range of branded goods, e.g. Sony, Zanussi, Dyson, Braun, and Philips.

Mail order – Next sells products directly to customers using a mail-order catalogue as well as its chain of shops throughout the country.

Internet sales and online shopping are now becoming the norm in addition to traditional sales outlets for some companies, e.g. Dixons, where in addition to high street shopping the same products are made available via websites with secure shopping on the internet.

Test your knowledge and understanding

12.1 The production process

1. Explain the meaning of the term 'production cycle'.
2. Describe the three main stages of the production process.
3. Name the functional area that has responsibility for the production of goods and services.
4. What is the production mix?
5. Choose a product and give an example of input, process and output.

12.2 Job, batch and flow production

1. Describe the key features of each of the main forms of production. Give the advantages and disadvantages of each.

12.3 Human versus machine

1. What are the benefits of human input?
2. What benefits are gained from using machines?
3. Why is the combined effort of humans and machines more effective than either on their own?

12.4 Quality control

1. Why is quality important?
2. Describe three quality models.
3. Give reasons explaining why stock control is important.
4. What is EPOS?
5. Describe just-in-time as a stock control system.
6. In what ways can ICT support stock control?

12.5 Methods of distribution

1. Describe five distribution options available to a business organisation.
2. Which distribution channel is a major growth area – and why?

Test your decision-making skills

1. Choose three goods/services. Prepare an IPO diagram for each.
2. Use ICT tools to prepare a graphical presentation on the elements of the production mix.

③ Create a table to compare the three methods of production. Use the following headings:

Method	Advantages	Disadvantages	Examples	Graphic

④ You own a small company producing specialist garden furniture. Prepare and present your case for using more people than machines.

⑤ As a result of unbelievable success your company cannot meet demand for your now famous garden furniture. How could you solve this problem and what difficulties might you encounter?

⑥ Prepare a leaflet for your class that highlights the main features of a quality model.

⑦ Suggest appropriate distribution channels for the goods/services you identified earlier.

What challenges face businesses?

In this unit you will learn about:

● competition at home and abroad
● the limited availability of resources
● internal and external pressures
● the effects of political, legislative, social and environmental issues.

13.1 Keeping up with the competition

'If you see a bandwagon to jump on, you are too late.'

Sir James Goldsmith, 1933–1997, multi-millionaire.

In any high street clothing shop, a quick look at labels will tell you that goods are made all over the world. No matter what the product is, e.g. sports socks, it can be, and will be, manufactured and distributed anywhere in the world. In these days of e-commerce, competition is no longer restricted to traditional sources – businesses now face competition from all angles. This will have a major impact on any business. You must 'match and beat' competition in order to survive and grow.

Elements of competition, i.e. areas where you must compete, will include the following:

● Price – will your price be higher/lower/special deals?
● Quality – will you focus on high quality?
● Delivery – timing/method/cost?
● Range of products – do you have a product family or a good range?
● Customer service – how does your service compare?
● Reputation – good image/poor image?
● Marketing/promotion – are customers more aware of you?
● Negotiations with suppliers/customers – are you good to deal with?

13.2 Limited resources

The term 'money doesn't grow on trees' is a well-known phrase. As individuals we are constantly faced with the dilemma of trying to match our limited resources to ever-increasing wants or demands on these resources. This leads us directly into making choices about how best to use these limited resources, the basic aim being maximum output from minimum input.

This principle applies to business as well as the individual. When businesses set out aims and objectives by strategic business planning, they are all subject to the issue of limited resources and competing demands.

- Land = all natural resources
- Capital = financial resources (amounts available for investment will be limited; machinery – quality, speed of production, types of machines – will be limited)
- Labour = employees (numbers and range of skills will be limited)
- Enterprise = the entrepreneurial vision may also be limited, depending upon the driving forces behind the business.

Case study

Production facility for Designer Caps

The owner of Designer Caps wants to expand the business. However, like any business owner, she faces the problem of limited resources.

Finance – financial resources are limited to funds available from investors or the amount that owners can justify borrowing from the bank.

Staff – in some ways you are limited by the skills, qualities and motivation of your staff.

Machines – your production capacity will be limited by the number and type of machines that you use. Should you wish to increase your production capacity then you will be required to invest (yes, that limited resource) in new production machinery.

Knowledge – the entrepreneur will need to have the vision to further develop the business. This is a limited resource and will depend on the knowledge and skills of the individual.

13.3 Internal and external pressures

Internal pressures are those which are generated from within the business. They are competing demands from different departments who will make a claim on resources to ensure that they meet their own objectives.

For example, the Production Department will continually try to improve production quality by investing in new equipment, while the Marketing Department will look for funds to finance new ways of promoting the good or service.

The business will have limited financial resources and must decide how best to allocate these to ensure that the business meets its aims and objectives.

External pressures

External pressures are those from outside the business and will come from a range of stakeholders.

- *Shareholders* – will be keen to see financial gains and growth.
- *Lenders* – will look for repayment and stability within the business thereby protecting their investment.
- *Suppliers* – payments must be made within agreed time limits.
- *Customers* – your goods/services must be sold to customers. Without them you have no business – therefore customers will put pressure on your use of limited resources to meet their needs
- *Competitors* – the more successful your competitors are, the more often resources available within the firm can be limited, since your customer base is declining and your income and funds for development will be even more limited.

13.4 / Other restrictions

Any business, no matter its size or type, operates under a range of restrictions that include legal issues, political agendas, environmental issues and social climates.

Legal

Legal issues will include laws that must be followed in relation to pollution of the air, water, noise, etc.

Employee/employer relationships are also covered by law, e.g.

Employment Relations Act 1999
Equal Pay Act 1970
Health and Safety at Work Act 1974
Race Relations (Amendments) Act 2000.

Laws are also in place to protect consumers, e.g. the Sale of Goods Act (1994). Goods must be as described, of merchantable quality and fit for the purpose.

Other restrictions include the scrutiny of advertising by the Advertising Standards Authority. This organisation looks at advertising campaigns to determine whether claims made are genuine or misleading. It also considers whether adverts may be offensive to groups in society.

Political

Political agendas will often influence and shape business activity. For instance, government economic management will influence investment, share prices, interest rates and international trade. Each political party, at national or local level, will have views that will influence decisions, e.g. planning permission for new buildings and licensing applications.

Environmental

Businesses, as well as individuals, are increasingly being asked not only to be aware of environmental issues but to actively consider environmental issues which may be impacted by their business activity, e.g. waste disposal; recycling and packaging.

It is worth noting that when businesses alter existing practices there is always a financial implication – again a combination of internal and external pressure on limited resources.

Social

Businesses are encouraged to show social responsibility and are often offered incentives by the government to locate their businesses in identified areas of social deprivation, providing investment and job opportunities in these areas.

When a large employer in an area is forced to close a factory, having a huge impact on the area, the government often step in, offering assistance either to the employer to help the business to stay, or to inject funds into the local economy to ensure the effects of the closure are minimised.

Businesses are encouraged to locate in areas of social deprivation

Test your knowledge and understanding

13.1 Keeping up with the competition

1 Explain the meaning of the term 'competition'.

2 Name and describe the areas where you must compete to succeed in business.

13.2 Limited resources

1 Why is it difficult to balance limited resources with unlimited wants?

2 Suggest four examples of limited resources.

3 Which resources were limited in the Designer Caps case study?

13.3 Internal and external pressures

1 Describe the main internal pressures faced by a business organisation.

2 Where might external pressures come from?

13.4 Other restrictions

1 Describe the legal restrictions that may influence business activity.

2 Why does the political climate affect business?

3 In what way do environmental issues influence decisions made by business organisations?

4 Should business have a social conscience? If yes, why? If no, why not?

Test your decision-making skills

1 As the owner of a sports shop, what can you do to match and beat your competitors?

2 Your business believes bigger is better – what factors may influence your vision of expansion?

3 Using a local organisation as an example, prepare a presentation of the main sources of external pressures facing the organisation. Choose from the following options:

   a presentation to class

   b handout to class

   c use presentation software.

4 Access the internet to find out details about the following:

- Employment Relations Act
- Health and Safety at Work Act
- Sale of Goods Act.

5 Find out how three multi-national companies actively ensure that they are environmentally-friendly.

Section 4

How businesses are managed

- What are the key decisions?
- What influences decisions?
- What aids decision-making?
- How are decisions made?
- How do businesses communicate?

In this unit you will learn about:

- what to produce (market research)
- what to charge (relationship between price and sales)
- who to employ
- where to produce
- interrelationship between the 4 Ps
- combining factors of production
- product life cycle.

14.1 / Market research

Knowing your market

In order to make the right decisions, businesses should be aware of their potential market. This can be determined by carrying out market research. Although this can be time-consuming and costly, it is better to establish solid foundations for future development.

Some methods of market research

Questionnaires

This method of information gathering can take many forms. A questionnaire is a series of questions designed to obtain a range of information on a given topic. Questionnaires can be postal, online, carried out door-to-door, carried out by a market researcher on the street, or by telephone.

Consumer panel

A consumer panel is where a group of customers are brought together to discuss possible products, changes, etc. It is designed to get as much information related to a decision as possible to ensure that the best decision is taken.

Hall test

This form of market research gathers a range of views about a new product, packaging, pricing, etc. by asking people 'in off the street' to gain their opinions.

Product tests

This form of market research gathers information from customers by letting them use the product over a period of time and then report back about their findings

Market research can also be split into two different types – desk research and field research.

Desk research

As the term suggests, information is gathered from existing sources – for example, looking at publications and figuring out trends from the comfort of your own office. You are more than likely these days to use the internet and electronic forms of information gathering. This tends to be used for gathering **secondary information** i.e. information gathered for one purpose and then used for another.

Field research

This type of research tends to be used when gathering **primary information** (fresh information gathered for a particular reason) and includes personal interview questionnaires. The benefits of this form of research are that the information you gather is designed for your purpose, it is up to date and it will be available when required.

14.2 Deciding on a price

When your market research is complete, you are faced with the challenge of deciding on your price level. This is a key decision, affecting both the immediate success of your product and ultimately the overall success of your business.

The pricing decision is influenced by a range of factors including the following:

- I want to make as much profit as possible.
- I want to keep my customers.
- I want to encourage new customers.
- I want to cover my costs.
- I want enough profit to reinvest.

The above factors highlight the complexity of choosing the 'right price' and illustrate that the price of your product or service cannot be looked at in isolation.

Supply and demand

The theory of supply and demand is an economic theory based on the relationship between prices and the demand for goods and services. The quality of goods that a company can sell to the consumer is called the **supply**. **Demand** is defined as the quantity of a product demanded at a given price at a given point in time. The basic law of demand states that when price is low, demand will be high; when price is increased, demand will fall.

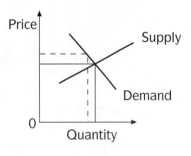

14.3 Reaching your target market

In business terms, your market is always out there – it's up to you to find your customers, reach out and capture them. Without them you are in trouble. No customers = no money = big problems!

Using the range of market research techniques mentioned earlier, you can find out as much as possible about your target market.

Example

An advertising agency runs a television campaign for a credit card.

It will analyse:

- requests for information from people who have seen the advert
- the customers who open an account
- where they transfer balances from and how much.

This will offer vital information for campaigns of the future.

Supermarket loyalty schemes

These provide an opportunity for supermarkets to analyse the purchases of individual customers in their stores and allow them to ensure they stock an appropriate range of products, and have the 'right' kind of special offers on a regular basis. Using this information they can match local needs, ensuring local success while contributing to the overall growth of the company.

14.4　Employment decisions

In Unit 12.3 we considered the balance of human versus machine. Here is a reminder:

Human

Machine

+	-	+	-
skill	wage costs	tirelessness	maintenance
brainpower	interdependence	accuracy	interdependence
problem solving	time limits	consistency	lack of flexibility
interaction	physical limits		
adaptability			

Human/investment costs

Whether you decide to employ more people than machines, i.e. become labour-intensive, or whether you decide to use more machines in production, i.e. become capital-intensive, you will consider a range of factors.

Either way there is a cost!

Capital-intensive production

If you are capital-intensive, as the name suggests, capital costs can be high. These are the costs associated with the purchase and installation of the machines or technology to take your organisation forward. Further costs to consider when you invest in machinery are the costs associated with training employees to use the machines. There is little point in investing £500,000 in a machine and leaving employees to figure out how best to use it!

Labour-intensive production

If you go down the labour-intensive route, costs can also be considerable. You must take into account the following:

- Recruitment costs – the time and money invested to ensure you get the right person.
- Training costs – ensuring employees are equipped with the necessary skills to complete work to the set quality standards.
- Replacement costs – if staff leave, or are absent on a regular basis, their work has still to be completed.
- Financial costs – all employees will need to be paid. Fewer employees = lower wage bills and vice versa! A downturn in business may lead to further costs if you have to make staff redundant, i.e. redundancy packages to pay staff off.

14.5 / The marketing mix

The marketing mix is described as the combination of the main elements of marketing; product, price, promotion and place (the four Ps).

Product

This is the good or service you offer to customers. Remember, goods and services include charities and public services. The product must be 'right' for its intended use. This refers to quality, image and availability.

Price

A key factor in determining the success of any good or service is price. Just how much is your good or service worth? The following are some methods of pricing adopted by different organisations.

When deciding on a price, all of these factors could come into consideration. There are six main methods of pricing products:

Cost plus

Work out what your product has cost to make and add on your profit margin, i.e. how much profit you want to make from each product you sell. For example, if your product costs £5 to make, selling it for £8 gives you a profit of £3 on every unit you sell.

Price matching

Price your product according to current levels in the market place, e.g. prices of CDs will be similar in a range of stores.

> **SUPA DEALS**
> We promise to beat the rest on price!

High-price strategy

Set your price level as high as you think the market will take with a view to presenting a quality image and gaining high profit levels.

Low-price strategy

Set your price at a lower level than your competitors in an attempt to gain more of the market – in other words, persuading customers to buy your product by appealing to their pocket!

Destroyer pricing

Set your prices at a very low level, often running at a loss in the short term. This is a method used in an attempt to gain entry into a market area that may be new to the business.

Skimming

This pricing strategy starts off at the top end of the market when a product is first launched. Once the product becomes established the price level is gradually reduced to make the product more readily available to a wider range of customers.

Promotion

Promotional activity supports the sale of goods and services. Advertising plays a major role here and is a topic we can all relate to. We look at and listen to advertising campaigns and either like them, hate them or have no opinion. Advertising is a very powerful tool in the promotion of any good or service.

The basic aim of an advert is to attract attention – other, more subtle, forms of promotion can then take over to persuade the customer that this is the product or service for them!

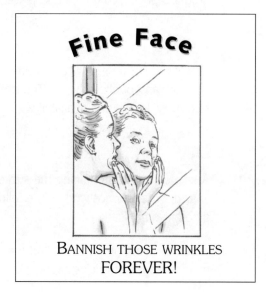

Fine Face

BANNISH THOSE WRINKLES
FOREVER!

Examples

- special offers
- linked offers
- competitions
- 3 for the price of 2
- collect tokens and send away for an item
- low-rate finance
- nothing to pay until 2005
- 12-hour spectacular sale
- window displays

The list goes on, but always remember the bottom line – the reason behind the promotion is to boost sales by attracting extra customers, and to keep these new customers.

Place

This is where the product is sold or made available for sale. This again presents a number of options.

Shops today are well-designed and attractive to customers for a purpose. Often the store is set out in a particular way with displays strategically placed to make shoppers think. After reading this you may look at shops differently – why is this here, why is that there?

Shopping centres are a development from traditional shops that link leisure facilities to shopping, thereby widening the experience.

A modern shopping centre

Internet shopping is another market for businesses – from cars to groceries to toys. Secure online shopping facilities are now commonplace, along with shopping carts and check-out icons, just like the real thing.

Mail order catalogues are yet another avenue used by companies. Customers use mail order catalogues to buy directly by phone and payments can be made in a variety of ways.

Summary

Consider the following example of the marketing of a holiday in Ibiza. Let's break down each area of the mix:

- *product* – hotel, apartment, quiet area, busy area
- *price* – varies – depends on accommodation, timing, length of stay
- *promotion* – TV, radio, newspapers, brochures, travel agent campaigns
- *place* – high street travel agent, internet, direct telephone booking.

This model can be applied to any good or service, clearly outlining the relationship between each element of the marketing mix, although the balance of the mix will differ with each good/service.

Combining the factors of production

Earlier we looked at the factors of production – land, labour, capital and enterprise. As in the marketing mix, we also have a combination of the factors of production.

The factors of production do not sit in isolation; they work together.

Case study

Wilson Sporting Goods

Wilson Sporting Goods are manufacturers of golf, tennis, and baseball equipment: clubs, rackets, bats, clothes, shoes, etc. We can see that land will be used for factories to produce the range of products, e.g. Wilson Sporting Goods, Irvine, produces golf clubs in the factory located there. In this factory they employ labour to produce goods, and capital is employed in the form of machinery to assist in this production. The enterprise comes from those who lead the business and develop the new technology, e.g. Wilson have launched a new range of golf clubs.

This is a brief example showing the combination of the factors of production land, labour, capital and enterprise working together, and the marketing mix kicks in on the strength of this.

Wilson has a product to promote, a price to establish, places to produce and outlets to supply, with the key objective of establishing a quality product in a competitive market, and ensuring that revenue exceeds costs.

14.6 Product life cycle

To be able to market its product properly, a business must be aware of the product life cycle of its product. A standard product life cycle tends to have six stages:

1. **Development** – research stage.
2. **Introduction** – the product has been developed and is launched.
3. **Growth** – the product becomes known and popular often leading to sharp increase in sales.
4. **Maturity** – the product is now well established and sales level off.
5. **Saturation** – all possible avenues have been explored.
6. **Decline** – at this stage the product is losing sales to competitors leading to a drop in sales and the product being taken off the market.

The product life cycle can also be shown in the form of a diagram:

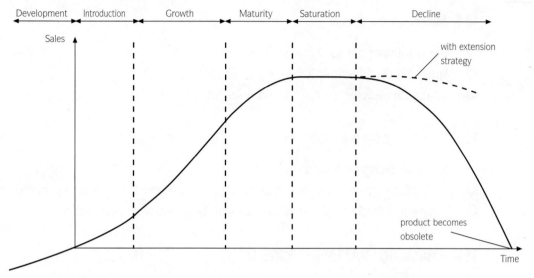

Product life cycle

Extension strategies

These are techniques to try to delay the decline stage of the product life cycle. The maturity stage is a good time for the company in terms of generating profit. During the maturity phase, the development costs of the product and the costs to establish it in the market are paid and it tends to then be at a profitable stage. The longer the company can extend this stage, the better it will be for it, i.e. more profit!

Some products have a short life cycle, e.g. fashion garments, whereas others have a much longer life span, e.g. KitKat biscuit – first launched in 1937 and still helping customers to have a break! Take a look at the KitKat website for a detailed history.

14.1 Market research

① Why is it important to 'know your market'?

② Name and describe four forms of market research.

③ Distinguish between desk and field research.

14.2 Deciding on a price

① Give a definition of demand.

② What effects may an increase in price have on demand for a good or service?

③ Prepare a diagram to show the relationship between price and quantity demanded.

14.3 Reaching your target market

① Why are advertising campaigns evaluated?

② How do businesses evaluate advertising campaigns?

③ How can supermarkets ensure they meet local customer needs?

14.4 Employment decisions

① Describe the meaning of:
   a labour-intensive production
   b capital-intensive production.

② What costs can be associated with labour-intensive methods?

14.5 The marketing mix

① Name and describe the main elements of the marketing mix.

② Give details of four methods of deciding on a price for goods or services.

③ Identify and give examples of ten forms of promotional activity.

④ What choices are available to businesses in terms of 'place'?

⑤ Give examples of products suited to different places.

⑥ Describe the factors of production.

⑦ Using Wilson Sporting Goods as an example, how do the factors of production combine to produce goods and services?

14.6 Product life cycle

① Name the six stages of a standard product life cycle.

1

  a What are the key elements of the marketing mix for this business venture?

  b How can Mr Jester keep in touch with his market?

2 Design a questionnaire to find out the top five films of all time.

  a Prepare your questionnaire using ICT and issue this to your class/group.

  b Analyse the results and present them in graphical form.

3 Prepare a report on a current advertising campaign from one of the following areas:

Health   Food   Clothing   Cars   Household cleaning

Present a summary of findings to your class.

4

A small knitwear designer produces 200 garments a week using a small number of machines and an equally small number of workers. As a result of a report in a designer magazine orders have increased dramatically.

What changes may have to be made should the designer choose to accept all of these orders? Give reasons for any proposed changes.

5

Investigate a range of products to establish the key elements of the marketing mix. Choose from the following examples:

Petrol   Supermarket
Sportswear   Computers
Holidays

Compare your findings with others in your class.

In this unit you will learn about:

- owner needs
- customer needs
- competition
- legal and social issues
- economic and political considerations.

15.1 / Meeting owner and customer needs

Owners of a business need customers to ensure the business survives, is profitable and meets its objectives. Clearly, if a business does not have enough customers a vicious circle begins. Costs will exceed income and the business will become unviable as an investment for the owner.

So owners of businesses must ensure they meet customers' needs. Customers' needs will, by now, be starting to sound familiar. Goods and services must be:

- the *right price*. What is the customer willing to pay – high, low, or market price?
- the *right quality*. Often the better the quality, the higher the price you can charge.
- *available*. If you cannot supply the goods/services, someone else will – your competitors!

Some other features that make up an attractive product are:

- *reliability* – the product must be fit for the purpose.
- *good design* – the design should be attractive and appropriate to the product.
- *image* – the product should create an image that appeals to the customer.

We can see that the relationship between customers and owners of businesses is very complex, hence phrases such as 'the customer is always right!'

15.2 / Competition

A competitor is any other business that offers the same goods or services as you, since it will be attempting to sell goods and services to the same target groups of customers. If your business is to be successful in terms of profit, growth or meeting objectives, then you must compete in the market place.

Mobile phones

The main networks for mobile phones are offered by BT Cellnet, Orange, One-to-One and Vodafone. They all offer a very similar service – a telephone network. How do they compete?

- price
- availability
- quality
- level of service

The price of the service changes continually, the quality of services will be improved on a regular basis, and the level and range of services will also change frequently.

As you will be aware, each of the mobile network providers is attempting not only to maintain its customer base but to increase this by attracting new customers, and persuading other mobile phone users to switch to its service.

If you think about the number of places you can buy a mobile phone, a similar pattern in terms of competition arises. All the different shops that offer mobile phones for sale also compete in the areas of price, level of service, quality and availability.

The clear message here is applicable to any business – if you do not consider your competitors and compete on price, quality and availability, your business will not survive!

If you are to win the competitive battle, you must be creative and be willing to take calculated risks.

If one store has a new promotional campaign, competitors tend to follow suit. The first company in will get the first opportunity to present information to potential customers. This is often referred to as being **proactive** – actively seeking to improve the present position.

Those who follow someone else's lead are described as being **reactive**. In other words they react to a situation and make decisions based upon a set of circumstances. If one holiday company offers free insurance, its competitors will react with a similar offer – they react to compete!

15.3   Legal and social issues

In Unit 13 we considered legal and social issues, and the impact that these have on business. In this Unit, examples will be used to highlight these areas.

Firstly, a brief reminder that laws are in place to protect employees, employers and customers. In addition to this, a range of laws protect the environment from pollution, etc.

But how do these **constraints** affect business?

The following business headlines will give you an idea of how legal and environmental issues must continually be addressed by organisations.

New cyber law comes into effect in China
A radical new IT act comes into force in China next week.

Leading petroleum company launches 'green awareness' campaign
Petroleum Worldwide has unveiled a new campaign to attract environmentally-aware consumers.

Examples of legal and environmental pressures on organisations can be found on a daily basis. Organisations must not only be aware of these issues, but should actively ensure that they work within the legal and environmental frameworks that exist.

15.4 Economics, politics and ethics

In this section, we consider the role of economics, politics and ethics and how they influence organisations.

Economics and politics

Organisations are affected by the economic climate and the political direction the economy is been steered towards. The following headline highlights political influences on business – this looks like a challenge from the government to business to boost economic development within the UK.

Chancellor challenges British business to raise production levels to compete with overseas rivals

Ethics

Ethics is difficult to define, but often the term 'doing the right thing' is used as a definition. Business ethics relate to businesses being encouraged, as the first headline below states, to act responsibly. The second example relates to job applicants who are encouraged to 'act responsibly' or be found out!

Business leaders call for ethical awareness plan

CV fraudsters face computer checks

Test your knowledge and understanding

15.1 Meeting owner and customer needs

1. What are owners' needs?
2. What customer needs must owners meet?
3. Describe the meaning of the term 'competition'. Give examples.
4. In what ways do the mobile phone networks compete?

15.2 Competition

1. In business it is better to lead than to follow – do you agree?
   If yes, why? If no, why not?
2. Explain the meaning of proactive. Give examples.
3. Explain the meaning of reactive. Give examples.

15.3 Legal and social issues

1. Give examples of legal constraints that affect business.
2. Give examples of political constraints that affect business.
3. Give examples of social constraints that affect business.
4. What is meant by business ethics?

15.4 Economics, politics and ethics

1. How can businesses be encouraged to act responsibly?

Test your decision-making skills

1. You are keen to become the owner of a state-of-the-art DVD player. As a customer, what are your needs?
2. You are a retailer of state-of-the-art DVD players. As a retailer, what are your needs?
3. You find out that your sales have fallen 10% behind your nearest rival. How might your business react to this situation?
4. How might you make your business more proactive?
5. Examine the market for soap powder to determine which brands are advertising new features.
6. The following extract looks at the impact of legal issues on business. Read the article 'Supermarkets slash medicine prices' and answer the following questions:

Supermarkets slash medicine prices

The price of over-the-counter medicines has been slashed by up to half in leading supermarkets following a High Court ruling lifting a law that fixed the retail cost.

The move is expected to save consumers millions of pounds, with Sainsbury's, Tesco and Safeway cutting the price of certain medicines and vitamins.

It could also prompt a fierce price war, with Boots already introducing a range of new promotions on medicines in an effort to stop supermarkets poaching its customers.

The ruling has been condemned by the Community Pharmacy Action Group (CPAG). It says the move could lead to the closure of 12,000 local pharmacies.

The Office of Fair Trading (OFT) challenged the price-fixing law – known as resale price maintenance – in the Restrictive Practices Court, arguing that it allowed drug companies to keep branded over-the-counter products artificially high.

New prices
Sainsbury's – 16 Nurofen now £1.14 from £2.29
Sainsbury's – Seven Seas Evening Primrose Oil now £2.79 from £5.59
Tesco – 16 Anadin Extra £1.29 from £2.15

CPAG had campaigned to keep RPM, arguing that high street chemist shops would lose business and be forced to close if the supermarkets launch price-cutting wars.

But the court found there was insufficient evidence that a significant number of pharmacies would be shut and ruled RPM was against the public interest.

Against public interest

The director general of the OFT, John Vickers, said: "This is excellent news for consumers who will now benefit from lower and more competitive prices for common household medicines."

But the outcome has been condemned as a "devastating blow" to Britain's pharmacies by CPAG's chairman and community chemist, David Sharpe.

"Many pharmacists will simply not be able to survive given the buying power and aggressive pricing tactics of the supermarkets," Mr Sharpe said.

"We continue to believe that we have a strong case and that many pharmacists rely on RPM to stay in business. However, having been given the clear indication that we are unlikely to win, it is in no one's interest to continue incurring further costs," he added.

The case was brought to the High Court last October by the OFT.

A spokesman for Boots said he was "disappointed" with the court's decision and estimated the move will knock £15m off full year profits.

Shares in Boots, the biggest chain of pharmacies in the UK, fell 4.5% on the news.

Source: BBC News Online (16 May 2001)

a What was the High Court ruling?

b What is meant by the term 'retail cost'?

c How do businesses arrive at this retail cost?

d Explain the meaning of the term 'price war'.

e Give some examples of promotional activity during a price war.

f Name the body that challenged the price fixing laws.

g What are the implications for independent chemists?

h How will this change benefit consumers?

i What problems may face retailers?

7 Search the internet for information on business ethics (business in the community, environmental issues, etc.). Helpful hint: try The Body Shop or Boots' websites to get you started.

In this unit you will learn about:

- how information helps decision making
- types of information
- a decision-making model
- the range of information used in decision making
- a complex decision-making model.

16.1 / The need for information

Business decisions must be based upon as much information as possible to ensure that the decision taken is the most effective and the best for the business. However, almost all decisions will contain an element of risk – there is no such thing as a guarantee! Any decisions taken will have an impact on the business and all angles should be covered when decisions are being made.

The decision-making process lies at the heart of the organisation and is always surrounded by a range of information. The following diagram shows how information surrounds the decision-making process.

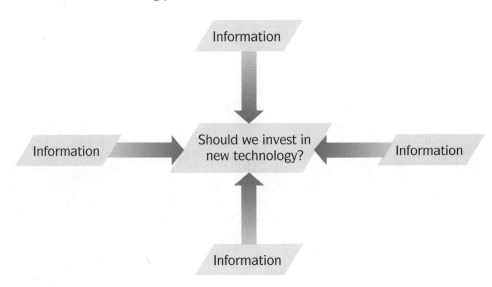

The information feeding into the decision-making process could include the following:

- Financial information – what are the costs and can we afford the investment?
- Training needs – how much training will employees need?
- Competitors – they have invested so should we?
- Cost/benefit analysis – will this make a difference?

These are only examples of the types of information that may be considered but information can be classified into specific types.

16.2 / Types of information

Information can be defined as processed data. Six types are as follows:

Primary information

This is information that is gathered for a specific purpose. Your business could commission some market research specifically designed to match a proposed change to a product. Sometimes it is described as first-hand information – clearly set up for your needs.

Secondary information

This is information that is gathered for one purpose and then used for another purpose. For example, your company may use the results of a national survey and take this into account when making its decisions. Sometimes secondary information is described as second-hand – it has not been designed for your needs, but you use the information as part of your decision-making process.

Internal information

This is information generated from within the organisation or business. It may take the form of financial reports, proposals regarding investment, marketing campaigns, etc.

External information

This is information generated outside the business, but that may be of value to the business such as economic forecasts, financial summaries for the market you operate in, or a review of buying habits of 14–18-year-olds, etc..

Quantitative information

This is information based on facts and figures. The information presented is factual and will not include judgements, e.g. 'there are 24 million mobile phones in the UK'.

Qualitative information

This is information that uses quantitative information to present an opinion, e.g. 'the most popular colour for training shoes is blue'. Obviously, this is an opinion based upon information; however, it is only an opinion and can be argued with.

16.3 / The decision-making model

A decision-making model is the method or structure followed by the person/business making the decision.

Brekkie Pops or Startrite Flakes?

Do you follow a model if you are shopping for breakfast cereal? You stand in the supermarket, look at the choices and decide which cereal to take off the shelf and put into your trolley – is this a model? Yes!

- Recognise need – no breakfast cereal at home.
- Meet need:
  - visit supermarket
  - make choice (think about factors influencing choice)
  - buy
  - evaluate decision (did you enjoy the cereal?).

Ways of making decisions

Decisions can be taken in a range of ways. If you operate as a sole trader, perhaps working on your own, then you are the person who makes all the decisions, basing them on your judgement, knowledge and experience.

In a larger business more people can be involved, sharing knowledge, experience and judgement. This gives more people the opportunity to look into and discuss issues before decisions are taken. It would seem likely, but it is not always the case, that this would give a more informed decision at the end of the day.

However, the more people you have involved in the decision-making process, the more time will be taken to reach decisions. There will be more scope for disagreement and some individuals may try to protect their position or look after their own interests when decisions are being taken.

Meetings

A simple model for decision-making is a meeting. A group of people get together to discuss an issue. Various points will be raised and discussed and an agreement reached. This agreement or decision will then be put into practice in the business and its impact will be monitored.

Another way of making decisions is consultation with your employees or, indeed, your customers.

Consultation – let's work together!

A proposal is drafted by the management team and put to the other employees in the business. The employees would then have the opportunity to put their views to management, and a final decision will be taken once all the views have been considered. The benefit here is that employees may take **ownership** of the  decision since they have been actively involved in the process. This being the case, employees will be more highly motivated and help the business achieve its goals.

Monitoring decisions

Remember businesses prosper or wither depending on the decisions they take. It is extremely important to take all relevant information into account, whether from internal or external sources – or indeed both. It is also very important to monitor the impact of the decision and this step should be built into the decision-making model. In other words, is the decision you made having the necessary effect? For example, if you decided to reduce prices to sell more goods, are you selling more? If so, how many more, and did the price change account for this?

Types of decisions

Organisations and businesses make three main forms of decisions:

Strategic decisions are usually long-term and have an effect on the entire business, e.g. a decision to merge/take over another company.

Tactical decisions are those decisions taken to move the business or organisation in a particular direction, tackling an issue or problem, e.g. a new promotional campaign.

Operational decisions are those taken to change existing procedures or to adjust the way activities within the business are carried out on a day-to-day basis.

16.4 / The range of information

If you are considering buying a new pair of training shoes you will take a range of information into account before making your decision.

● You will consider information on price – are the trainers the same price in all stores?
● You will consider information on the product – design, function, colour, fashion status, etc.
● You will consider alternative styles.

- Either consciously or sub-consciously, you will be influenced by advertising/promotional campaigns by the manufacturers/sellers of the trainers.

Obviously, a similar range of information will influence business decisions, but the range may be wider. Earlier in this unit we looked at the different types of information – each of these will influence a range of business decisions. Consider the following diagram:

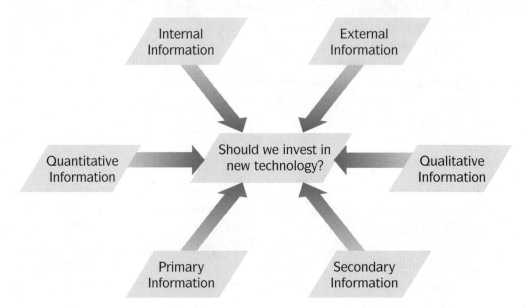

In a decision-making process this range of information could be referred to as the information mix. Different combinations of information will be required depending on the nature of the decision, e.g. whether it is strategic, tactical or operational.

Other factors that may influence decisions relate to the following:

- *Actions of competitors* – you may be forced into change as a result of decisions taken by competitors, e.g. new promotional offers.
- *Economic climate* – your decision may be influenced by external events, e.g. poor trading conditions, low spending by consumers etc.
- *Legal issues* – your decision may be affected by the law, e.g. the decision to stop pharmaceutical companies setting minimum prices for their products.

16.5 Complex decision-making

From the simple model to the ten decision-making commandments!

Given the range and complexity of factors that influence decisions, a more comprehensive model could be adopted. In this model we can adopt ten separate stages in the decision-making process.

① *Identify the problem* – what is the source of the problem?

② *Identify the objective for the solution of the problem* – what do you hope the solution will achieve?

③ *Identify the constraints* – what factors may prevent you from being able to solve the problem?

④ *Gather information* – get as much information as possible to ensure you make the best possible decision: primary, secondary, internal, external, qualitative and quantitative.

⑤ *Evaluate alternatives* – look at all possible solutions.

⑥ *Select the best possible solution* – pick the solution that most suits present circumstances within and outside the business.

⑦ *Inform those involved* – ensure that all involved or affected by the solution/decision understand forthcoming changes.

⑧ *Sell the decision to those involved* – make sure that you do all you can to 'sell' the benefits of the decision to all concerned: employees, customers, shareholders, etc.

⑨ *Implement the solution* – put your decision and any changes into practice throughout the business.

⑩ *Monitor and evaluate your solution* – make sure you look at the effect of your chosen solution/decision; has it worked?

The following example takes you through a complex decision-making model.

Step	Example
Identify the problem	Sales have fallen over a three-month period
Identify objective for solution of problem	Increase sales levels
Identify constraints	Competition Finance for new advertising Limited range of products
Gather information	Combination of desk and field research to get to reasons for change in sales
Evaluate alternatives	New advertising campaign Adjust prices Endorsement by personality
Select best possible solution	New advertising campaign
Inform those involved	Range of staff from Marketing/Finance/Sales
Sell decision	Ensure all staff know what is happening, why it is happening and anticipated outcome
Implement	Launch new campaign
Evaluate	Analyse results of campaign – have sales increased?

16.1 The need for information

❶ Why is information important when decisions are being made?

❷ Are decisions ever risk free? Give reasons for your answer.

❸ What kind of information may you take into account when making decisions?

16.2 Types of information

❶ Give a definition of information.

❷ What is primary information?

❸ How does secondary information differ from primary?

❹ What is meant by internal information?

❺ Give a description of external information.

❻ What is quantitative information?

❼ How does qualitative information differ from quantitative information?

16.3 The decision-making model

❶ Explain the meaning of the term 'decision-making model'.

❷ Suggest four stages in a simple model.

❸ Describe two ways of making a decision.

❹ Give the advantages and disadvantages of each method.

16.4 The range of information

❶ Identify and describe three kinds of decisions that may be taken by a business.

❷ Explain the meaning of the term 'information mix'. Give an example to illustrate your answer.

❸ What factors may influence decisions?

16.5 Complex decision-making

❶ List ten possible steps in a more complex decision-making model.

Test your decision-making skills

❶ You are responsible for a new marketing campaign. What information do you think you might need – and where might you find it?

❷ Find five business news stories/headlines. For each one make a note of the decisions that have been made.

❸ For each of these stories/headlines, identify the range of information that could have been used. Remember the range includes primary, secondary, qualitative, quantitative, internal and external.

❹ Choose a durable good that you have bought (or been bought) recently – can you build a simple decision-making model relating to this purchase?

❺ Using a complex decision-making model, follow each step to build up the example:

Your production costs have risen …

You have just lost your key sales person to your nearest competitor …

How are decisions made?

In this unit you will learn about:

- consensual versus authoritarian management
- the impact of management style on motivation and morale
- the characteristics of effective management.

Management styles

Dictator or team?

Decisions are made on a regular basis and in
different ways according to the nature of the
business or the decision itself. We can consider the
spectrum of a decision-making model by looking at
the two extremes.

Authoritarian

At one end of the scale you have an authoritarian style of decision-making. In this model
the decision is taken by the 'boss'. The person in charge will make the decision based

upon his or her views. This method will provide a speedy
decision – it may be based upon experience, but will
often lead to frustration on the behalf of employees who
have not been consulted. The knock-on effect is that
employees will not have the same belief in the decision
since they have not been involved in the process.
Whether the decision proves to be correct or not, time
will be taken to win over the employees when decisions
are taken in this manner.

Consensual

When decisions are made using a consensual approach, a more team-oriented approach is
adopted in an attempt to ensure that the right decision is taken and appropriate changes
implemented within the business. At this end of the scale decisions taken go through a
series of consultation processes whereby the views of the employees are sought.

Employees are more likely to be actively involved in the decision-making process. More people are involved, more information is made available and considered, more avenues explored, therefore a logical conclusion would be that a 'better' decision would be taken. Since employees are involved, they are more likely to support the decision and take issues forward since they will have 'ownership' of the decision and will be motivated to ensure that 'their' decision works.

A term often used to describe this form of management is **empowerment** which means giving employees power to make decisions since they are centrally involved and affected by the decisions they make.

17.2 The impact on staff and efficiency

The varying styles of management used within a business organisation will clearly have an impact on the people who work in that organisation. Organisations have to weigh up which style is appropriate for their business.

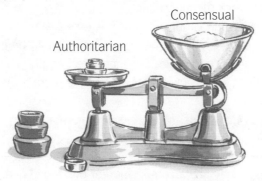

Some employees will feel comfortable and perform well in an authoritarian environment. A simplistic view is that if they follow instructions and are not part of the management or decision-making process then they have to bear less responsibility for the decision ('I was merely following instructions, your honour.'). No matter what happens, or what their opinions may have been, they are not to blame if things do not go according to plan. The type of employee described here would tend to be less highly motivated – a follower rather than a leader.

At the other end of the spectrum there are employees who are regarded as being central to the decision-making process and key people within the organisation. Just consider the different impact on motivation. At this end your views not only count, but may well shape the direction of the company. Your motivation would be greatly increased since you and your colleagues would take a sense of 'ownership' of the decision, giving it your full support and thereby helping the business achieve its goals – a set of goals that you have helped to shape.

Bearing these extremes in mind, we can start to tackle the concept of effective management.

Management has many definitions – but here's one to work with which is very straightforward.

Management is getting work done through delegation of tasks to others. A key feature of this definition is how the work is delegated in the first place.

Effectiveness also has many definitions – a starting point would be ensuring that tasks are completed in the best way possible depending on the circumstances at that point in time.

From these basic definitions what makes an effective manager? If a manager is to be successful or effective then he or she must possess certain skills and qualities.

- *Leadership qualities* – the ability to 'take people with you'.
- *Communication skills* – making sure that people get the message.
- *Organisational skills* – making sure that what should happen does happen.
- *Motivational skills* – encouraging people to perform at their best.
- *Planning skills* – setting out tasks to be completed and considering all angles.
- *Interpersonal skills* – working with a range of personalities, ensuring that the 'right' approach is adopted for the individual.
- *Listening skills* – this sounds obvious, but it is essential that a manager listens.
- *Experience* – you learn something new every day – bank the experience!
- *Adaptability* – ensuring that you can change direction/people/focus as necessary.
- *Presence* – sometimes you know that the person is there – they have the personality!
- *Vision* – to boldly go …
- *Decision-making skills* – gathering all relevant information and making decisions (often tough decisions that impact on staff).

At any point a manager may use a combination of the above qualities/skills; the range will depend on the situation. So let's tackle the question – how do you measure an effective manager?

Here are some options:

- Compare targets with actual results e.g. target 5% increase in net profit, achieved 10% – does this indicate success?
- Relationships – getting the job done often leads to conflict along the way. Do working relationships under the direction of the manager survive the stresses and strains of tough decision-making to ensure the business meets its targets?
- Long-term views – is the success or the change sustainable over a longer period of time. Your 5% increase may result in ongoing costs that may lead to major problems!

Some food for thought:

- Good managers get results – that's all that counts.
- Good managers are born not created.
- Good managers do not become bad managers overnight.
- A good manager is someone who can look, listen and decide.
- A good manager values opinions.

Test your knowledge and understanding

17.1 Management styles

1. Describe how decisions are taken if an authoritarian style is adopted.
2. What are the benefits to employers/employees if an authoritarian approach exists?
3. Describe how decisions are taken if a consensual style is adopted.
4. What are the benefits to employers/employees if a consensual approach exists?

17.2 The impact on staff and efficiency

1. What might be the impact on employees' motivation in a business where all views are considered important?

17.3 Effective management

1. Identify and describe five key qualities of an effective manager.
2. Describe three ways of 'measuring' an effective manager.
3. Good managers are born not created. Discuss!

Test your decision-making skills

1. 'Required – tough decision-maker to lead the business through dramatic changes.' What management style would be required, and why?
2. 'All For One, And One For All plc – new Managing Director required to take business forward. Please note our name sums up the way we work as a unit.' What kind of management style would be most successful for this company, and why?
3. You feel that your staff depend on you too much. What steps could you take to increase their independence? How would this benefit the business?
4. Identify people you see as leaders/managers and then complete the table below. Use software as appropriate.

Name	Business/Organisation	Reason(s)

In this unit you will learn about:

- formal and informal communication
- internal and external communication
- the effectiveness of different communication methods
- using ICT.

18.1 / The importance of effective communication

In earlier units we established the central role of information in any business organisation. A natural follow-on is that the communication of information is a key issue in determining the success of the business organisation.

The better the quality of information that flows around the organisation, the better the chances of the 'right' decisions being taken. We have established that information is used to:

- inform stakeholders of current events and future plans
- inform and persuade customers/potential customers
- make decisions.

Let's look at communication in more detail – yet another key feature!

Examples of communication

Communication takes many forms – here are four examples.

Written communication

Any information that is presented in a written/ printed format is described as written communication. Examples are business reports or letters.

Visual communication

Every picture tells a story! Often we can look at the same things and see them so differently, hence the expression 'you only see what you want to see'.

When products are pictured in catalogues, magazines, brochures, etc. a great deal of time, effort and money will be invested to ensure that the 'correct visual impact' is achieved and in turn passed on to potential customers.

Verbal communication

Any verbal interaction is described as verbal communication. Examples are conversations, discussions during meetings, telephone calls, etc. – all rely on the spoken word. Verbal communication should be clear, well-structured and concise. We all speak to a range of people on a daily basis, and still messages get mixed up. How often have you heard, or indeed said, 'I thought you meant ...'.

Body language

This form of communication refers to the way in which you communicate via your body. It includes posture, gestures, movement of the body during verbal communication, how you sit on chairs, etc..

From these examples we can quickly establish that this communication business is very complex, and made even more so when you start to mix and match the methods.

18.2 Mixing methods of communication

When a new product is being launched on to the market a promotional campaign will include a mix of the forms of communication discussed above.

- Written communication in the form of a slogan/message to customers.
- Visual communication – posters/billboards, videos, advertisements.
- Verbal communication – dialogue from radio/TV advertising campaigns.

Different products will require different combinations depending on the nature of the goods/services being promoted.

We can take the example a stage further by considering the difference between a television and a radio advert. In the TV version, visual communication is supported by verbal communication in an attempt to get the message across. It would seem much more difficult to do the same with a radio advert on its own, relying solely on verbal communication.

Business organisations communicate more effectively if they mix their methods of communication to ensure that the all-important message is delivered to its target audience.

Formal and informal communication

Communication can also be split into formal and informal methods.

Formal communication is a planned activity and specific to a set purpose. An example of where formal communication takes place is a meeting of the board of directors of a company. This meeting will follow a set **agenda** and a record will be kept for future reference. Written reports would also be regarded as examples of formal communication.

Informal communication is a situation where issues are discussed, but no prior planning has taken place. Examples of informal communication are discussions over coffee and social chat that may include discussions relating to the business.

Again, a mix of communication methods and styles will be used by business organisations, but the way in which you communicate may differ depending on whether the information being organised is for use within the business or for external purposes.

Internal and external communication

Internal communication is meant for use within the business, e.g. memos, e-mails, notices, reports, etc. The purpose of the communication will determine the quality requirement; a quick memo for distribution to all departmental managers is an example of internal written communication. A sales report for discussion by the sales team is also an example of internal written communication but the quality requirements are completely different, i.e. the difference between a quick note and a discussion paper.

External communication is designed for use by people/groups outside the business, e.g. a company's annual report, bid for a contract, business plans, etc. Again, external communication methods will contain a mix of written, visual and spoken forms of communication.

Barriers to effective communication

- *Quality of information* – poor quality information can lead to ineffective communication. If you design a poster based on poor market research, then no matter how good the poster might be, the communication will still be poor.

- *Delivery of information* – getting the message over. If it's communicated at the wrong time or wrong place, the message does not fulfil its purpose.
- *People* – you see what you want to see, you hear what you want to hear – sounds familiar? People take (and give) what they interpret, and interpretation is never easy (just ask your English teacher!).

Clearly, ineffective communication can be very frustrating!

18.3 Information and communications technology (ICT)

A further factor to consider when looking at communications is the role of information and communications technology. The recent information explosion has been made possible by the ever-developing use of ICT as a business communications tool.

E-mail

This is a computer-to-computer messaging service with built-in ability to send and receive electronic messages and files via computer networks. Businesses may send e-mail bulletins to potential customers advertising their products.

Internet

The internet has become an amazingly powerful tool to buy, sell, advertise and research new products. With all these tools we have seen incredible growth in e-commerce. This has provided business organisations with opportunities to expand their horizons, e.g. your weekly shopping can now be done from the comfort of your own home via the internet. Just wait for the delivery – after you have paid of course!

Web cam/video

This facility offers the ability to see and hear others via computers fitted with cameras, software and linked via computer/telephone networks. This use of ICT reduces the need for people to travel to meetings, saving both time and money.

Voicemail

There is no need to continually redial numbers – leave a message and wait for a reply!

Mobile phones

The mobile phone has made instant communication so much easier, and with the power of the mobile, internet connections and text-messaging services are now an assumption rather than being regarded as high-tech luxury. Indeed, text-messaging services now have their own language as well as the predictive text technology supporting their use.

Video-clips via computer

Mini-videos promoting products are now available online in addition to brochures. Just imagine how much a holiday company could save if it printed fewer paper copies of brochures – never mind the impact on the environment!

As with a number of areas covered in the 'mix', ICT methods will vary according to the needs of the business and the nature of the tasks.

Test your knowledge and understanding

18.1 The importance of effective communication

❶ Name and describe four common forms of communication.

❷ Give examples to illustrate uses of each form of communication.

18.2 Mixing methods of communication

❶ Why does a mix of communication methods give better results?

❷ What is formal communication?

❸ How does informal communication differ?

❹ What is the difference between internal and external communication?

❺ Why might the presentation quality of information used for external purposes be greater than that used internally?

18.3 Information communications and technology (ICT)

❶ What are the benefits of e-mail as a means of communication?

❷ How can the internet be used as a communication tool?

❸ Describe the key advantages of voicemail systems used in businesses.

❹ How have mobile phones broken down communication barriers for businesses?

❺ What opportunities do the use of web cams/video conference facilities open for a business?

Test your decision-making skills

❶ Name your three favourite adverts. For each one describe the message behind the advert.

❷ For each advert analyse the communication involved. Prepare a table to show your findings:

Product	Description	Written	Visual	Spoken	Body Language

❸ In your position as Global Communications Director for a software firm, what would your strategy be for both internal and external communications for your business? Give reasons and examples to support your strategy.

Index